RESOLVING

BUSINESS

DISPUTES

The Potential of Commercial Arbitration

AUTHORS

Steven Lazarus

John J. Bray, Jr.

Larry L. Carter

Kent H. Collins

Bruce A. Giedt

Robert V. Holton, Jr.

Phillip D. Matthews

Gordon C. Willard

RESOLVING BUSINESS DISPUTES

The Potential of Commercial Arbitration

AMERICAN MANAGEMENT ASSOCIATION
NEW YORK

331.15
34.1

This is No. 85 in the series of AMA Management Reports. It has been distributed without charge to AMA members enrolled in the General Management Division. Those members who are enrolled in other divisions, or who wish extra copies, may order the Report in a hardcover edition at $6 per copy. Price to nonmembers, $9.

This book was originally prepared as a research report submitted in partial fulfillment of the requirements for the Manufacturing Course at the Harvard University Graduate School of Business Administration. The conclusions and opinions expressed herein are those of the authors and do not necessarily represent the views of the Harvard Business School, Professor Georges F. Doriot, or individuals, business firms, associations, or government agencies contacted. Having from one to ten years of business experience (or related experience in the military) prior to attending the Harvard Business School (1963-1965), the authors conducted extensive original research preparatory to writing this book.

Library of Congress catalog card number: 65-24369

TO

GENERAL GEORGES F. DORIOT

President,
American Research and Development Corporation

Professor of Industrial Management,
Harvard Business School

FOREWORD

This book is the product of extensive research into the process known as commercial arbitration. At the outset, we recognized that financial and time constraints would prevent the achievement of statistical depth; therefore, we attempted to develop the broadest possible spectrum of current attitudes concerning arbitration. To this we added much library research and our own creative thought. We hope that our judgments and findings will provoke interest and perhaps constructive controversy. We consider the book to be not an end but a beginning.

We must express special thanks to Professor Georges F. Doriot, who challenged us to reach beyond the limits of our conventional aspirations; to Professor James J. Healy, who helped, guided, and encouraged us; and to Mr. Donald B. Straus, and the entire staff of the American Arbitration Association, who provided invaluable assistance and who patiently responded to every request for information and clarification. Many other individuals took time from busy routines to respond to questionnaires, to submit to interviews, or to read portions of the manuscript. Their contributions to our work were significant, and it is with regret that we can only thank them collectively.

THE AUTHORS

PREFACE

Settling disputes by arbitration is as old as the submission of the quarrel among Aphrodite, Hera, and Athena to the judgment of Paris. Yet arbitration has also been thought fitting in the most modern commercial contexts, both domestic and international. The recent proposal by the World Bank for a convention on arbitration of investment disputes is an example of the new uses to which the technique may be put.

In this volume the authors review the utility of commercial arbitration for solving twentieth-century business problems. They consider the relative value of arbitration in different business situations, pointing out those conflicts in which it can and cannot be used to advantage. They evaluate legal criticisms of the process, recommend certain changes in the conduct of proceedings, and make some predictions as to the course arbitration may take in the future. The subject is approached from several points of view, including those of businessmen, lawyers, judges, educators, and arbitrators. Readers from each of these callings should benefit. Those who now know little about commercial arbitration should acquire useful familiarity with the subject.

Although neither I nor anyone else would agree with all the positions taken by the authors, RESOLVING BUSINESS DISPUTES illuminates an important subject and deserves the interest of the business community.

JOHN T. CONNOR
Secretary of Commerce

CONTENTS

CHAPTER I

THE CURRENT STATE OF
COMMERCIAL ARBITRATION •

THE PRESIDENT of a rapidly expanding electronics company faces two problems. First, he depends upon a key supplier for a steady input of highly sophisticated and expensive electronic components. Each of these components is tested upon receipt. If they do not meet certain electronic specifications, they are unacceptable. However, the threshold of unacceptability is, to a great extent, a matter of subjective judgment. The president is in a quandary, for if he refuses to accept certain components and returns them without payment, his supplier could stop deliveries. This could necessitate a shutdown of production. On the other hand, if he accepts questionable components he jeopardizes the quality of his finished product. Disputes over the quality of the components could be taken to court, but during this period he would achieve little or no production. He could argue the matter privately with his supplier, but this could be time consuming and there would be no guarantee of successful resolution. What can the president do?

Second, this same company licenses its systems for use abroad. It recognizes that when dealing with such a complex mechanism as an electronic system the potential for disputes over quality of performance is great. The president is concerned about the distances, differences in language and customs, and misunderstandings which could complicate the resolution of such disputes. He is aware that should negotiations fail, international litigation can be a long, involved, and often unrewarding alternative. Furthermore, he is very interested in maintaining his relationship with his foreign licensee and does not desire to see that relationship clouded and possibly ruptured as a result of an unresolved dispute. Since his systems embody considerable proprietary technology, he wishes to avoid being required to expose them in detail in a public court proceeding. What can the president do?

In each instance Mr. Franklin A. Lindsay, president of Itek Corporation, alleviated his problem by employing an arbitration clause in his purchase and licensing contracts. However, he is part of a minority of businessmen who know about and successfully use commercial arbitration.

Commercial arbitration is a method of resolving disputes between businesses by submitting such disputes to the binding decision of a third person, usually another businessman who has a technical competence in the matter in question. The situations described above are not unique, and similar problems arise in many businesses. When business disputes occur, they are often aggravating and sometimes damaging. Any solution which can prevent the aggravation and minimize the damage should be welcome. The purpose of this book is to reintroduce the businessman to commercial arbitration.

Arbitration, particularly in its commercial form, is both old and tested. Some of the more lyrical writers on the subject, when attempting to fix its historical origin, make sweeping reference back to the mythical judgment of Paris (which allegedly helped to bring about the Trojan War). Arbitration, in its modern and practical form, has had more constructive and less provocative results. For example, in the field of labor-management relationships arbitration is employed extensively, and grievance arbitration machinery has become an essential part of the labor agreement in American industry.[1]

The use of arbitration to resolve accident claims disputes has expanded rapidly, and insurance companies have become the largest users of non-labor arbitration. Two organizations of insurance firms, the American Insurance Association and the National Association of Mutual Casualty Companies, arranged for arbitrators who settled 19,036 automobile insurance cases involving member companies in 1960, 2681 more than in 1959 and more than triple the total in 1954.[2] Between 1960 and 1963, the figure doubled to 38,313, and arbitrations were being conducted in 98 cities throughout the country.

Compared to the successful and widespread employment of labor and accident claims arbitration, commercial arbitration has had a relatively slow growth and has achieved only a limited acceptance among the business community. Since commercial arbitration is the most venerable of modern-

---

[1] S. H. Slichter, J. J. Healy, E. R. Livernash, *The Impact of Collective Bargaining on Management* (Washington, D.C.: The Brookings Institution, 1960), p. 745.
[2] *The Wall Street Journal*, May 23, 1961, p. 1.

day arbitration methods, it seems worthwhile to investigate the reasons for its present level of use and to determine whether or not there are areas in which it could be gainfully employed.

WHAT IS COMMERCIAL ARBITRATION?

Beyond the dictionary definition of commercial arbitration,[3] there are several aspects which require illumination and clarification. Commercial arbitration must be understood as a specific entity, entirely separate from what is called labor or industrial arbitration and from a new and burgeoning field known as accident claims arbitration. The differentiation between commercial and international trade arbitration is not one of kind but of locality; therefore, they will be treated as two parts of a single subject. Finally, commercial arbitration must be seen in an historical perspective in order to understand its potential for the future.

LABOR ARBITRATION AND ACCIDENT CLAIMS ARBITRATION

The pervasiveness of labor arbitration is a relatively recent phenomenon and is worthy of brief examination in order to place commercial arbitration into proper perspective. Prior to World War II, little use was made of the arbitration mechanism in solving disputes and settling grievances between management and labor. The advent of hostilities, however, made both the strike and the lockout inimical to the war effort and critically dangerous for public policy to tolerate. Knowing that differences would not evaporate but in all likelihood would be aggravated under the pressures of accelerated production, the Government had to develop an alternative

[3] Definition of Arbitration: Act of arbitrating; esp., the hearing and determination of a cause between parties in controversy by a person or persons chosen by the parties, or appointed under statutory authority, *instead of by a judicial tribunal provided by law;* the hearing and determination of a matter of dispute by an arbiter or arbitrator. The matter may be submitted by an agreement, usually called a *submission,* to one arbitrator, or to two, who are to choose a third called an *umpire,* or to an arbitral board or court. The decision given is called an *award.* At common law, arbitration is entirely voluntary, and a submission to arbitration is revocable by either party, or avoided by his death, before the award is duly made. Arbitration may be: (1) *international,* whereby disputes between sovereign states may be settled, as by the Hague Tribunal or by the Permanent Court of International Justice; awards are now commonly binding, esp. if given by a permanent court or if so agreed by provisions of a treaty (arbitration treaty); (2) *industrial,* whereby disputes between employers and employees may be settled, and (3) *commercial,* whereby disputes arising out of contracts, business transactions, etc., may be settled out of court by a specially established tribunal. By permission of *Webster's New International Dictionary,* Second Edition; © 1959 by G. & C. Merriam Company.

method of resolution. The National War Labor Board was created to administer this alternative. It offered industry a choice—voluntary arbitration by mutual agreement or compulsory arbitration under the Board.[4]

Although labor voiced alarm and dissatisfaction with certain phases of the War Labor Disputes Act (Smith-Connally Act), which clearly established the fundamental source of the War Labor Board's authority, it firmly supported the concept of arbitration. A banner reading, "The Arch Saboteur of Our War Effort is the Unresolved Dispute—Use Arbitration" was hung at the foot of the rostrum in full sight of the thousands who attended the Southern War Labor Convention of the American Federation of Labor held in Atlanta on January 16 and 17, 1943.[5]

The war proliferated the use of labor arbitration, facilitated the wide acceptance of the principles of arbitration by labor and management, and vastly increased use of arbitration clauses in collective bargaining agreements.[6] It is significant that arbitration was resorted to and successfully used during a time of crisis and that enforced familiarity with it led not to contempt but to its continued and increased employment.

There are basic differences between labor arbitration and commercial arbitration. The current form of labor arbitration is similar to the mediation activities of the medieval craft guilds. (However, the functions of mediators and arbitrators are different. The mediator traditionally directs his efforts toward bringing the positions of the disputing parties together, actively participating in their negotiations, and attempting to effect a compromise acceptable to both. Arbitration is a judicial process where the parties agree to accept as final and binding an arbitrator's decision, made after the arbitrator receives and evaluates evidence.)

Labor arbitration is normally the final step in a formal multi-step grievance procedure. Labor arbitrators are paid whereas commercial arbitrators, customarily, are not. However, the most significant difference between the two forms of arbitration concerns the intimacy of their relationship with the law. Matters referred to both labor and commercial arbitration are justiciable. Under modern statutes, the courts will hold the agreement to arbitrate to be valid and will enforce the award as a judgment of the court. But such statutes are seldom applied to labor arbitration.[7]

---

[4] *Arbitration in Action,* Vol. 1, Nos. 7-8 (July-August 1943), p. 17.
[5] *Arbitration in Action,* Vol. 1, No. 2 (February 1943), p. 16.
[6] J. S. Murphy, "An Outline of a Course in Labor-Management Arbitration," *The Arbitration Journal,* Vol. 16, No. 3, 1961, p. 120.
[7] F. A. Kellor, *Arbitration in the New Industrial Society* (New York: McGraw-Hill Book Company, Inc., 1934), p. 134.

The potential threat of legal economic coercion in the form of strikes and lockouts is enough to make the parties to a labor arbitration subordinate themselves to the process. Such economic necessity also operates, to a degree, in the functioning of trade-association commercial arbitration; therefore, the results of such arbitration do not normally require enforcement by law. But the circumstances which motivate the actions of trade association members do not apply in the majority of commercial arbitration cases. Characteristically, commercial arbitration derives its vitality and power from the modern arbitration statutes. The most important single influence on commercial arbitration is its complex involvement with the law.

The New York compulsory automobile insurance law of 1956, as amended by article 17-A, created the Motor Vehicle Accident Indemnification Corporation (MVAIC). The purpose of the coverage was to provide some protection for innocent people who were involved in accidents with uninsured motorists. One of the conditions of the system was that, should the corporation and the insured be unable to agree on legal liability and/or the amount of damages owing, the determination should be made by arbitration.[8] This provision gave great impetus to the employment of arbitration for the settlement of accident claims in New York State; and, in general, the use of accident claims arbitration is burgeoning throughout the country. It is significant that arbitration is here being successfully employed to provide a remedy in a situation where before there was no adequate means of recovering monetary compensation for damages caused by financially irresponsible motorists. It is also significant that arbitration is being successfully employed in an area where the number of cases is already vast and growing at an accelerated pace.

HISTORICAL OVERVIEW: THE EVOLUTION OF COMMERCIAL ARBITRATION

The Greek city states of the sixth, fifth, and fourth centuries B.C. used the process extensively for settlement of disputes concerning boundary delimitation, ownership of colonies, ownership of particular pieces of territory, assessment of damages suffered through a hostile invasion, in recovery of money owed by one state to another, and in all sorts of religious matters. It was a common practice to insert in treaties a clause providing for settlement by arbitration of disputes arising in the future among the parties to the treaty.[9] In the early Anglo-Norman period, it is difficult to dis-

---

[8] Gerald Aksen, "Uninsured Motorist Coverage: A Guide to MVAIC and Arbitration," *The Arbitration Journal*, Volume 15, No. 4 (1960), p. 178.
[9] Gertrude Smith, "The Greeks Had a Word for It," *Arbitration in Action*, Vol. 1, Nos. 4-5 (April-May 1943), p. 5.

tinguish between jury determination and arbitration proceedings. What was termed litigation was often a mediating effort on the part of the court to effect an acceptable honorable compromise. The courts had a well-developed conception of the essential attributes of a valid arbitration proceeding, and the jury system itself developed as an outgrowth of the arbitral concept.[10]

The Merchant's Law (Lex Mercatoria), or at least the codification of it, apparently originated in the thirteenth century, for the dealings of merchants necessitated the use of simple rules. It was necessary that there should be expeditious settlements of disputes and summary executions to enforce decisions between buyers and sellers, who were strangers to each other and who dispersed to distant places when their transactions were over. Much of the commerce in the Middle Ages was carried on at great fairs, and it became a matter of course to attach to every market a Piepoudre[11] Court for the purpose of swiftly deciding disputes as to contracts concluded or broken within the market.[12] Such a court consisted of a businessman, a town official, and a third person (not an attorney); it could be considered the ancestor of the modern arbitration panel.

Legal commentary indicates that the acceptability of arbitration was dealt a severe and possibly unwarranted blow by the dictum pronounced in 1609 by Lord Edward Coke in Vynior's case. Lord Coke said "that though one may be bound to stand to the arbitrament yet he may countermand the arbitrator . . . as a man cannot by his own act make such an authority power or warrant not countermandable which by law and its own proper nature is countermandable." According to Cohen,[13] in Coke's day the arbitrator was not a judge whose purpose it was to find on the merits of a controversy but was merely an agent attempting to effect compromise. Thus the doctrine of reversibility of the arbitrator's decision seemed proper.[14] Even though the trend in the courts is currently away from the principle of revocability, this doctrine continues to have some modern-day

---

[10] Daniel E. Murray, "Arbitration in the Anglo-Saxon and Early Norman Period," *The Arbitration Journal,* Vol. 16, No. 4 (1961), p. 193.

[11] The word could be translated as "dusty feet," and it was said that such courts derived their name because disputes were settled before one could shake the dust of travel from his feet.

[12] Julius Henry Cohen, *Commercial Arbitration and the Law* (New York: Appleton-Century-Crofts, 1918), p. 75.

[13] *Ibid.,* p. 95.

[14] Daniel Bloomfield (ed.), *Selected Articles on Commercial Arbitration* (New York: The H. W. Wilson Company, 1927), p. 6.

acceptance among attorneys, as does the widespread impression that arbitration is still synonymous with compromise.

The very considerable eclipse of arbitration as an accepted and widely used form of settling disputes lasted for over 300 years. Arbitration continued to be confused with compromise and bargaining, and litigation emerged as a sovereign remedy for conflict. The law evolved a system of courts, a body of precedent, a professional ethic, and a group of brilliant and articulate exponents. Arbitration fell into disuse. One commentator conjectures that discord and dispute were complacently accepted in nineteenth-century America where conflict seemed healthy, resources seemed endless, and profit margins were high enough to allow considerable waste. Self-regulation seemed unnecessary.[15]

The tide seems to have begun to turn with the trial of *Scott versus Avery* in the House of Lords in 1855. Lord Chancellor Cranworth, who presided, observed that the latitude for unilateral revocability on the part of one party to an arbitration was "an inconvenient . . . irrational . . . and absurd state of the law." Lord Campbell, in *Russell versus Pellegrino,* commented, "Somehow the courts of law had in former times acquired a horror of arbitration; and it was even doubted if a clause for a general reference of prospective disputes was legal. I never could imagine for what reason parties should not be permitted to bind themselves to settle their disputes in any manner on which they agreed. The decision in *Scott versus Avery,* that an agreement that there should be a reference before the party should be at liberty to sue might be so made as to be binding, was a very wholesome decision."[16] The effect of these cases and others was persuasively presented in a 1918 study by Julius Henry Cohen *(Commercial Arbitration and the Law).*

It is difficult to identify the pertinent trends and changes which were occurring in early twentieth-century America. Certainly, there was a growing industrialization, the westward expansion was over, World War I had produced a tremendous convulsion in national and international awareness, the Pan American experiment was taking place, and the League of Nations had been created. There were new forces at work in the land and new attitudes toward conflict. In 1920, the State of New York enacted a modern arbitration law, the first of its kind in the United States. The enactment of this law was due largely to the initiative taken by the New

---

[15] Frances A. Kellor, *American Arbitration* (New York: Harper and Brothers, 1948), p. 6.
[16] Cohen, *op. cit.,* p. 180.

York State Bar Association, to the support given by the Chamber of Commerce of the State of New York and other commercial organizations, and to the influence of Cohen's book.[17]

There was considerable interest in commercial arbitration during the 1920's. The U.S. Congress passed an arbitration law. The American Arbitration Association was founded. Most of the influential arbitration literature was written during this period. Since this time, interest seems to have waned and waxed intermittently. The period of intense interest in labor arbitration during and after World War II has been noted, as has the application of arbitration to the disposition of accident claims in the 1950's and 1960's.

Currently, the use of commercial arbitration is increasing at the rate of about 10 percent per year, but it is very difficult to judge to what extent it is being employed compared with its useful potential. It is unknown to or at least poorly understood by a large percentage of businessmen. Some part of the legal profession remains hostile to its use. Conversely, the interest of and participation by attorneys in it seems to be growing. This seems to be prompting a growing institutionalization of commercial arbitration leading toward a final and full accommodation with the law.

THE ELEMENTS OF COMMERCIAL ARBITRATION

At first, the commercial arbitration process seems extremely simple—a neutral decides a dispute between two opposing parties. However, to the businessman the process means one thing, to the arbitrator another, and to the attorney a third. Actually, commercial arbitration is an amalgam of all three viewpoints. A problem exists because each participant—businessman, arbitrator, attorney—often understands commercial arbitration only as it relates to himself, to the exclusion of other viewpoints. A greater problem potentially exists in that the viewpoints of the participants are so in conflict that sooner or later one must dominate. If this is so, the final problem remains: Which viewpoint will gain ascendancy?

THE BUSINESSMAN

The businessman is one of the three key participants in the arbitration process. He is attracted to arbitration because he is a practical man

---

[17] Kellor, *op. cit.,* p. 10.

who is interested in doing business. He has little reason to be fascinated with the strategy of conflict. His goal is the resolution of conflict, and he desires to effect such resolution in the most expeditious manner possible. In the words of William G. Caples, vice president, industrial and public relations, Inland Steel Company:

> . . . use of an arbitration clause to provide for the peaceful settlement of future disputes is not unusual. Every business transaction contains the seed of disagreement, error or difference of opinion. Partnership agreements; contracts for the employment of professional or executive personnel; agreements covering patents and licenses; and contracts for the sale or purchase of goods; rentals of space or equipment; or construction or renovation of facilities—these activities, so common that they are taken for granted, can easily lead to controversy. The sums involved may be comparatively small or they may zoom into millions. Often, no monetary claim is made; the dispute may concern specific performance of a contract. The arbitral process gives both sides an opportunity to resolve difficulties quickly, privately and economically. The average case can be completed in two or three months. . . .[18]

Revenue is achieved through a smoothly functioning trade relationship, and such a relationship is normally disrupted by a business dispute. Therefore, arbitration is seen by the businessman participant as a forum for quick and practical resolution of business disputes. The importance of the businessman to commercial arbitration cannot be overstated. The process exists strictly for him, and his sponsorship and endorsement is a critical requirement if commercial arbitration is to be successfully perpetuated.

THE ARBITRATOR

The arbitrator is usually a businessman or an attorney who has, for the purposes of arbitration, assumed another role. The arbitrator does not serve for economic reasons. Except for unusually long cases, the commercial arbitrator is not paid, or at least not more than a token amount. A survey, conducted by the authors, of arbitrator attitudes indicates the arbitrators participate because they believe that arbitration is a logical area in which to discharge one's social responsibility. They believe that arbitration exists only because of a willingness on the part of two parties to submit a dispute to the binding decision of a third. To the arbitrator, this connotes a higher, more civilized form of human activity, and he finds it esthetically reward-

---

[18] William G. Caples, "Keeping the Peace in the Business Community," *Commerce,* July 1964.

ing to participate in such a forum. This, once again, is a broad generalization, and interesting differences in arbitrator motivation will be discussed in Chapter III. However, it is not unreasonable to say that to most arbitrators, commercial arbitration is viewed as a form of high social responsibility. The future of commercial arbitration depends on the quality and competence of the arbitrators. More than any other single group, the arbitrators control the ultimate success or failure of the process.

THE ATTORNEY

Perhaps the least easily understood aspect of commercial arbitration is the role of the attorney. We have seen that the process originated outside the common law system in the Lex Mercatoria, and vestiges of this resistance to attorneys remain in the trade associations. The antipathy of some attorneys to the commercial arbitration process will be discussed in Chapter IV. It is obvious that the accommodation of the legal profession to arbitration is by no means comfortable or complete. The lawyer participant brings to arbitration an awareness of the adversary nature of the proceeding and an awareness of the fact that a modern arbitration statute is required in order to prevent unilateral revocation of an agreement to arbitrate future disputes. The presence of the attorney is a reminder that where such enforcement machinery does not exist, the willingness of a party to submit voluntarily has been known to falter. The lawyer naturally brings to arbitration his legal frame of reference and his desire for carefully institutionalized procedure. This has prompted a trend which one commentator has called "creeping legalism." More important, however, is the fact that the lawyer participant views arbitration as a forum where two adversaries meet in conflict. The attorney is a permanent member of the arbitration triumvirate. He is no more dispensable than the businessman or the arbitrator. His presence is a reminder that the voluntary character of an agreement to arbitrate is far stronger in the general sense than in the particular case and often gains effect not through submissive behavior on the part of the parties but as a result of the law which stands behind it.

ARBITRATION AGENCIES

To what extent is commercial arbitration being practiced today? This question cannot be answered by simply totaling up the number of cases handled by the American Arbitration Association. There are many trade associations and at least one international body practicing a very successful form of commercial arbitration, and in several of these the mere existence of a commercial arbitration mechanism over the years has facilitated the ease of face-to-face settlement between the disputing parties. Disputes settled through direct negotiation under the influence of a commercial-arbitration-conditioned environment might well be considered in an evaluation of the use and influence of commercial arbitration. However, there is little statistical information in this area.

AMERICAN ARBITRATION ASSOCIATION

The American Arbitration Association was founded in 1926 as a combination of two prior organizations, the Arbitration Society of America and the Arbitration Foundation. Frances Kellor, in her book *American Arbitration,* describes the merger as an integration of two differing factions, one progressive (the Foundation) and one conservative (the Society). Participating as honorary presidents were Charles Evans Hughes, Charles T. Bernheimer, Herbert T. Hoover, Newton D. Baker, and Moses H. Grossman.

It is not our purpose to detail the history of the American Arbitration Association. It is important, however, to note that it actively advanced the process of arbitration, developed a wide base of advisory support through industry and the business community, established 17 branch offices, constructed national arbitration panels with over 18,000 members, and codified standard arbitration procedures. In 1940 it was named administrator of a special system of arbitration instituted under a consent decree to which the U.S. Government and five major motion picture distributing companies were parties. When labor arbitration became the only means to sustained labor-management peace during World War II, the American Arbitration Association was called in to assist the War Labor Board in administering this hugely expanded activity.

In 1956 a statistical study by the University of Chicago of commercial cases held under the auspices of the American Arbitration Association concluded with these comments:

> From this general study of 545 cases arbitrated at the American Arbitration Association . . . [it is shown] that the American Arbitration Association is an important commercial tribunal and that arbitration is a faster method of adjudication than courts. The study also shows that the American Arbitration Association arbitrators are apt to be experts in the matter involved. . . . although there are many questions yet to be answered, it is

clear that the American Arbitration Association plays a major role in resolving commercial disputes in many industries [and that] whether because of the speed, economy or expert justice of the American Arbitration Association arbitration, or all three, these industries indicate their satisfaction with the tribunal by continuing to bring their disputes to the American Arbitration Association.[19]

Most of the cases coming before the American Arbitration Association have been initiated under an arbitration clause in a contract between the parties involved. However, it is not essential that arbitration be decided upon before the advent of a contract or dispute. Agreement by the parties to arbitrate their differences does occur after the dispute has arisen but is less common than initiation through an arbitration clause.

The standard American Arbitration Association clause is the instrument most frequently used and is normally written into the commercial contract. It reads as follows:

> Any controversy or claim arising out of or relating to this contract, or breach thereof, shall be settled by arbitration in accordance with the Rules of the American Arbitration Association, and judgment upon the award rendered by the arbitrator(s) may be entered in any court having jurisdiction thereof.[20]

The scope of this clause is to include any disagreement or dispute that is considered arbitrable under the law and by the parties involved. While there are certain other legal limitations on the arbitration process and its scope, the clause is an integral part of the contract and consequently court action is usually required only when the legal effectiveness of the contract or the contract's legality itself is questioned.

The arbitration clause normally indicates the agency to handle the arbitration and the rules under which the matter will be settled. In the standard American Arbitration Association clause, the American Arbitration Association will handle all administrative tasks; and its rules in effect at the time of the dispute will be used in the proceedings. Matters may be brought to arbitration in either of two ways. *Submission:* Voluntary acceptance of arbitration can be made by filing of such statements by both parties with the American Arbitration Association. *Demand:* Where a future disputes-clause is in effect, one party may give notice of his intention to arbitrate

[19] Hal M. Smith, "Commercial Arbitration at the American Arbitration Association," *The Arbitration Journal,* Vol. 11, No. 1 (1956), p. 20.
[20] *Commercial Arbitration Rules of the American Arbitration Association,* as amended and in effect June 1, 1964 (New York: by the American Arbitration Association).

by filing such notice at American Arbitration Association headquarters. The other party may file an answer. If no answer is filed, it will be assumed that the claim is denied. If the respondent refuses to participate, the proceedings may go forward ex parte. An award granted under such a proceeding is valid and may be given effect in court.

When named in such a clause, the American Arbitration Association becomes the administrator and performs all administrative functions involved in carrying out the arbitration.

The appointment of an arbitrator or arbitrators is accomplished in accordance with current procedures. A list of names from the American Arbitration Association arbitrator panel is given to each party, and they may cross out objectionable persons, indicate a preference in terms of priority, and return the list to the American Arbitration Association. The Association then invites the arbitrators, in the order mutually agreed to by the parties, to accept the case. In some agreements the selection of one arbitrator is made by each of the parties, and the American Arbitration Association appoints a third, neutral arbitrator acceptable to both parties. However, unless otherwise stated in the agreement, only one arbitrator is selected, in the manner described by the American Arbitration Association procedures.

Upon the selection of the arbitrator, the time and place are fixed for the hearing by him. This and all other communications are handled by or through the American Arbitration Association. The arbitrator is normally not paid for his services, but an administrative fee is required by the Association and is related to the amount of the claim.[21] In order to keep down expenses, a transcript of the hearing is not made unless it is specifically requested.

Under the American Arbitration Association rules, the arbitrator may, and usually does, open the hearing by the filing of an oath. Administrative details, such as the recording of the date, time, place, persons present, are accomplished. Normally, statements clarifying the issues are then given by both sides. The complaining party presents his case, followed by the defendant. The arbitrator has discretion to vary this procedure, with

---

[21] *Ibid.*

Amount of Claim	Filing Fee
Up to $10,000	3% (Minimum $50)
$10,000 to $25,000	$300 plus 2% of excess over $10,000
$25,000 to $100,000	$600 plus 1% of excess over $25,000
$100,000 to $200,000	$1350 plus ½% of excess over $100,000
Over $200,000	Discussed with Amer. Arbitration Assn. before filing.

his only limitation being a requirement to give equal opportunity to all parties for presentation of any material.

The arbitrator has full and sole responsibility for the interpretation of the arbitration rules as to his own powers. His powers with regard to postponements, adjournments, and reopenings are quite flexible in that he can modify the timing to provide for the individual circumstances and reasonable requests of the interested parties. Independent inspections can be made by the arbitrator as long as the parties are notified of this intent and of the time so that they may be present if they so desire. Conformity with legal rules of evidence is not necessary, and the arbitrator is the judge of relevancy and materiality of the evidence offered.

After the hearing of evidence is completed and all parties conclude the presentation of their cases, the arbitrator has normally (unless otherwise specified in the agreement) 30 days in which to render an award. If more than one arbitrator is used, the decision must be by majority. In any event, the award must be in writing but need not present the reasons for the decision. The arbitrator may grant any remedy or relief which he deems just and equitable, provided such power is not specifically restricted in the contractual agreement or by law. This may include a full settlement, require specific performance of the contract, or such other remedy as the arbitrator deems proper. The award must, however, indicate which party must pay the expenses of the arbitration (unless it is otherwise provided for in the contract). One of the most significant aspects of the award is that there is currently no appeal mechanism for reviewing the arbitrator's decision under the usual American Arbitration Association procedure.

Today, the American Arbitration Association occupies a full floor of modern offices at 140 West 51st Street, New York City, and maintains branches in 17 other cities: Boston, Massachusetts; Charlotte, North Carolina; Chicago, Illinois; Cincinnati, Ohio; Cleveland, Ohio; Dallas, Texas; Denver, Colorado; Detroit, Michigan; Hartford, Connecticut; Los Angeles, California; Miami, Florida; Philadelphia, Pennsylvania; Pittsburgh, Pennsylvania; San Francisco, California; Seattle, Washington; Syracuse, New York; and Washington, D.C. It now supervises approximately 1,200 commercial arbitration cases annually.

TRADE ASSOCIATIONS

The term "trade association" is difficult to define precisely. It can mean anything from a loosely federated, vaguely related group of companies to a tightly knit, intimately connected industry. There are approximately 2,000 associations represented on the roles of the American Society of Association Executives, and approximately 63 of these provide facilities for arranging arbitration. Many employ the facilities of the American Arbitration Association. Others, such as the General Arbitration Council of the Textile Industry, are affiliated with the American Arbitration Association but incorporate in their regulations certain modifications to American Arbitration Association procedure. Many others operate independently.

Arbitration within trade groups has existed for centuries. A pure form of commercial arbitration was developed under the English craft guilds, which originated in the twelfth century. Such a form covered all transactions among members belonging to a particular craft.[22] These crafts jealously guarded their powers to enforce their decrees and awards; throughout the years, their decisions accumulated and developed into a code of conduct and ethics. As a rule, such instruments of self-government specifically excluded and resisted the introduction of ordinary, external legal procedure and, by implication, those voices of the law, the attorneys.

Our research has not attempted to survey the entire range of trade-association arbitration in the United States. Our sample, however, has revealed a number of characteristics which may be considered indicative. The arbitration procedure of the New York Stock Exchange is a case in point.

Arbitration on Wall Street was formally established in 1817 and has been working successfully ever since. In a business where millions and even billions of dollars worth of transactions are effected daily by merely a telephone or other verbal order or consultation, it was immediately recognized that the money involved in such transactions could not and should not be interminably tied up in extended litigation and that expeditious adjudication of any dispute was absolutely essential to the conduct of the business.[23]

The Exchange's arbitration facilities are available as a service to the Exchange's membership and to the public. These facilities are used most frequently to dispose of disputes between Exchange members and their customers. Individuals in the securities business and persons outside of the securities field serve voluntarily as arbitrators. A five-man panel hears every case. By agreement between the parties, the decision of the arbitrators is final. There is no requirement that the parties be represented by

---

[22] Clarence F. Birdseye, *Arbitration and Business Ethics* (New York: Appleton-Century-Crofts, 1926), p. 16.
[23] Max Jaquin, Jr., "Arbitration in Action in Wall Street," *The Arbitration Journal,* Volume 1, No. 3 (Fall 1946), p. 262.

counsel, and in many cases they have no attorney. Arbitrators are traditionally paid for their services, but the amount is nominal and payment is more symbolic than remunerative. It is significant that most disputes are settled without the necessity of having to resort to the arbitration process.

Generally, our survey of trade associations yielded six important points.

1. An industry which by nature requires a close continuing relationship among the members seems to gravitate to the use of arbitration. The New York Stock Exchange is one example. Mr. Edward Fuller, of Greenwood Mills and the General Arbitration Council of the Textile Industry, says that in the textile industry salesmen are trained in the art of repeat selling. Therefore, there is a necessity for continuing relationships; mutual confidence and goodwill are important.

2. An industry in which the quality of the product is a matter for interpretation is susceptible to commercial arbitration. In addition to the textile industry, this characteristic is exemplified by the American Cotton Shippers Association, the Association of Food Distributors, and others.

3. There was a general rejection of attorneys. Even the textile industry, which employs them to represent the parties to a dispute, forbids them as arbitrators. The maritime industry excludes them. The American Spice Trade Association does not use them "99 percent of the time." This phenomenon will be discussed further in Chapter IV.

4. There are disparate views on the payment of arbitrators. An official of a nationally known business association feels that "a day's work should be dignified by a day's pay." A representative of the textile industry says, "If you pay, you'll get hacks who are always available." Under the procedures of the National Canners Association, the arbitrator is paid $10 for each dispute. Maritime industry arbitrators are also paid. However, the sample size is too small to allow any statistically based judgment as to which view prevails.

5. A number of associations have established appeal boards which can be solicited to review the judgment of an arbitration tribunal. These exist in the Spice Trade Association, the American Cotton Shippers Association, and the maritime industry.

6. Perhaps the most significant characteristic is the general acceptability of arbitration within the surveyed associations and the decrease in the number of cases as the "arbitration habit" is incurred and the procedure becomes familiar. This trend was pointed out explicitly by the Association of Food Distributors, the National Association of Grain and Feed Dealers, and the National Canners Association.

INTERNATIONAL BODIES

International Chamber of Commerce Court of Arbitration. The International Chamber of Commerce Court of Arbitration, headquartered in Paris, was inaugurated on January 19, 1923. On that occasion Mr. Etienne Clementel, president of the Court, said in part:

> Strict justice, however, has the very defects of its qualities: this equity, this impartiality demand on the part of the judges a much closer examination of the matters in hand, all the more so as those being judged are a long way from their judges. The procedure will therefore of necessity be longer when it is a question of settling an international dispute. The two parties will be put to a certain amount of expense and, owing to delays, may suffer from a locking up of capital which may cause them considerable inconvenience. Moreover international disputes usually bear on questions of a technical nature, which can only be settled by a technical expert. The judge will therefore have to consult an expert and in many cases his opinion will determine the award. It is therefore natural that businessmen and practical men of action have considered it possible to have direct recourse to such an expert not by appointing him as arbitrator themselves but by having him appointed by an international organization, which they have elected, the decision of which they have agreed to carry out. They are of the opinion that it will save them a great deal of time and money . . . .[24]

Since its creation, approximately 5,000 parties have been involved in the 2,000 disputes submitted to the I.C.C. Court. Among the bodies active in the field of international commercial arbitration, the court is the only one which makes itself available to the business community not only without national or territorial restrictions but also regardless of the nature and subject of the disputes submitted to it. The unique and universal nature of the I.C.C. Court is suggested by perusal of a handbook drawn up by the United Nations Economic Commission for Europe dealing with the main national and international arbitration institutions in Europe and the United States. This document lists 93 specialized institutions which restrict their activities to one product and lists 31 centers dealing with general arbitration but created for the requirements of the foreign trade of a specific country. I.C.C. arbitration therefore complements specialized arbitration. For example, the Havre Cotton Market stipulates recourse to the I.C.C. Court of Arbitration for all disputes other than those concerning the quality of the goods. Disputes involving quality are arbitrated within the

[24] International Chamber of Commerce, "Brochure No. 22, Inauguration of the Court of Commercial Arbitrations January 19, 1922" (Paris: International Headquarters, 33 Rue Jean-Gonjar, 1922), p. 16.

trade.[25] A more detailed discussion of the workings of the I.C.C. Court of Arbitration is contained in Chapter VI.

Other institutions. As indicated above, there are a great many specialized and nationally oriented arbitration agencies operating outside the United States, with which an American businessman may occasionally find himself involved. For example, most contracts between the Soviet Union and private businessmen provide for arbitration in Moscow of disputes arising under the contract. However, it is beyond the scope of this report to analyze the operation of each of these agencies. Chapter VI will attempt to provide a broad enough discussion of the characteristics of international-trade arbitration to permit anticipation of most of the problems incident to it.

The World Bank, in Washington, D.C., has developed an international arbitration mechanism, which it intends to administer itself, to apply specifically to disputes concerning foreign investment.

The United Nations sponsors two organizations which, among other functions, operate to facilitate and promote the practice of commercial arbitration although they do not supervise arbitration themselves. These are the Economic Commissions for Europe and the Economic Commission for Asia and the Far East (ECAFE). ECAFE has established a center for promotion of commercial arbitration, which lists its functions as follows:[26]

1. *Collection and dissemination of information* including pamphlets and brochures, technical data on arbitration clauses, institutional arrangements, rules of procedure, and so forth.
2. *Technical assistance,* including services of technical advisors to assist in the establishment of national facilities and arrangements for the training of local personnel.
3. *Research activities* consisting of legal and technical studies relevant to the improvement of arbitration in the ECAFE region. This work is to be carried out in close cooperation with the existing national and international agencies concerned with arbitration.

THE CURRENT CONTEXT

In order to understand commercial arbitration, it is necessary to understand the modern context in which it exists. Of the four facets of that context described below, two relate specifically to commercial arbitration:

[25] United Nations Economic Commission for Asia and the Far East, *ECAFE Center for the Promotion of Commercial Arbitration News Bulletin* (November 1964), p. 30.
[26] *Ibid.,* p. 38.

the geographical concentration of commercial arbitration cases, and the conciliatory effect which familiarity with the process seems to have on certain antagonists. The other two facets relate to the general economic environment: the effect of crowded court calendars evident in certain areas, and the effect of the increasing volume of international trade.

GEOGRAPHICAL CONCENTRATION

There is little question that New York City has long been the heart of commercial arbitration in the United States. Of the 3,858 commercial arbitration cases conducted by the American Arbitration Association during the period 1961 to 1964, 2,522 were held in New York City. There are a number of reasons for this. New York State enacted the first important, modern arbitration law in the United States; the paradoxical characteristic of modern commercial arbitration is that in most instances it requires the existence of a law in order to be successful. Second, New York has been the major locus of trade in the United States, and up until the present, it has been those disputes incident to trade (as opposed to manufacturing), such as those involving somewhat subjective judgments concerning quality, which seemed most amenable to commercial arbitration. Third, many of the original arbitration clauses specifically called for arbitration in New York City. This is still the case in the textile industry; although the issue has become something of a bone of contention, Mr. Fuller, of the textile industry's General Arbitration Council, supports the policy as follows: "The textile market is in New York and all manufacturers are represented here. This is the largest concentration of knowledgeable people, and it is relatively easy to obtain a wide selection of arbitrators."

This phenomenon of geographical concentration has probably restricted the spread of commercial arbitration. Businesses operating outside the influence of New York City had little occasion to be exposed to commercial arbitration, and, as Mr. Fuller says, nowhere else can as large a concentration of knowledgeable people be found. This observation not only applies to expertise in the textile business but also applies to expertise in arbitration itself. There are indications, however, that pressures are building which will ultimately change this situation.

STRANGENESS VERSUS FAMILIARITY

Related to the geographical nature of commercial arbitration is the fact that familiarity with the subject usually leads to acceptability, and strangeness sustains suspicion. As one commentator puts it, many an attorney approaches arbitration "like a lonesome cat in a strange alley." In connection with our research, the deans of 75 schools of law and graduate schools of business administration were contacted by the authors. Of the 43 schools which replied, 19 reported that the subject of commercial arbitration is touched upon in courses in contracts, remedies, and so on. However, the average time devoted is one to two hours per semester. Several respondents believed that the use of commercial arbitration would not increase because some sections of the legal profession regarded it with suspicion and that such suspicion could be allayed only through education and exposure. Dean Orlando John Hollis of the University of Oregon School of Law comments as follows:

> My opinion is that the arbitration mechanism will probably become more generally used as more experience is gained with the procedure and its availability becomes more generally known . . . . The growing understanding on the part of many businessmen and their lawyers that competent arbitration boards may be able to understand much more easily and more quickly the problems involved than can a jury of inexperienced and uninformed laymen . . . will provide the basis for . . . an increased use of the mechanism.

However, there is little doubt that resistance to commercial arbitration exists. A respondent reports: "I was interested to learn that the chief counsel of one of the two corporations for which Professor Jones [name disguised] worked had a uniform rule that attorneys in the corporation's legal department should not include arbitration provisions in contracts to which the corporation was a party."

The reasons for such resistance are not capricious and go far deeper than the historical antecedents discussed previously. These reasons will be examined at length later. But the evidence of satisfaction in the trade associations and the results of our surveys and interviews, which also will be discussed at greater length in succeeding chapters, indicate that many of the reservations concerning commercial arbitration are dispelled or at least minimized through exposure.

A WORD ABOUT THE COURTS

In many areas, crowded court calendars have caused grave concern among legislators, jurists, and attorneys. In the civil court of New York City, delays involving tort jury cases ranged from 33 months to as high as 50 months.[27] Where a separate commercial docket exists, delays are usually shorter—approximately nine months. However, lengthy discovery proceedings can extend this significantly. One New York attorney described as not unusual a business dispute case that has taken two years to get through the pretrial investigatory period.

The incidence of crowded dockets is directly related to the geographical considerations described above. Not all dockets are crowded; not everywhere is there a delay in court. But in the great commercial centers the problem is swiftly becoming acute, and as these centers spread and merge into vast megalopoli, the severity of the problem can only increase.

INFLUENCE OF INTERNATIONAL BUSINESS

International-trade arbitration has for many years been employed successfully for the settlement of international business disputes. As indicated above, however, most international arbitration bodies are specialized or national in character. The International Chamber of Commerce has long advocated greater compatibility among national procedures and more universal commitment to reciprocal enforceability of arbitration awards. In 1958 the United Nations convened an international conference on enforceability, and this conference drafted a convention on the subject. The United States did not sign this convention.

There are many factors which suggest that a review of the U.S. position concerning international commercial arbitration is in order. The amount and complexity of international trade is increasing at an accelerated pace. Many American corporations, such as Singer Company, are becoming transnational in nature. Regional economic groupings such as the European Economic Community complicate the already tortuous entanglements associated with international commercial litigation. Developing nations are beginning to challenge the traditional arbitration machinery. Russia and the bloc nations use arbitration to the exclusion of all other methods in the settlement of business disputes.

These and other factors indicate that the influence of international business is of primary importance to the future of commercial arbitration and that commercial arbitration would have a profound influence on the future of international business. This will be explored more fully in a later chapter.

[27] Summary of 1964 Report of the Senate Judiciary Committee (State of New York), Macneil Mitchell, Chairman.

* * *

The use of commercial arbitration has increased more slowly than the use of labor and accident claims arbitration, even though the latter two are relatively new phenomena and commercial arbitration dates back to the ancient Greeks. Perhaps this is, in part, a result of the tripartite and contradictory nature of commercial arbitration which seems to embrace elements of practicality, social responsibility, and conflict. Legal antipathy to commercial arbitration dates back to 1609 when Lord Coke saw arbitration as attempting to "oust the jurisdiction of the courts." However, increased participation by attorneys in arbitration, particularly in American Arbitration Association proceedings, seems to be effecting some modifications of this antagonism. This participation is also tending to make the arbitration procedure more legalistic in nature, and this trend is being resisted by the trade associations.

The geographical concentration of arbitration activity has undoubtedly inhibited its spread. To many attorneys the mechanism has remained a strange and foreign procedure and, therefore, not to be trusted. However, it originated as a businessman's answer to a businessman's problem, and the future of commercial arbitration may once again be in the hands of the businessman. Crowded court dockets, which bottle up commercial disputes sometimes for years, have prompted businessmen to seek an alternative. But even more important are the potential uses of arbitration as American business moves increasingly into the international sphere. Existing international arbitration bodies function, and new ones are being created; but thus far the United States has played a relatively passive role in international arbitration.

If the future of commercial arbitration depends on the businessman, it depends most particularly on his role as sponsor, on his activity as arbitrator, and upon the structure of his relationship with his attorney. If the businessman is to sponsor commercial arbitration, he must be able to see practical value in it. It is, therefore, important in the following chapter to determine what the businessman actually does know and think about commercial arbitration. It is perhaps even more important to provide the businessman with an unbiased picture of the applicability of commercial arbitration in order to assist him in forming his own conclusions concerning the potential use of the process.

CHAPTER II

THE BUSINESSMAN AND COMMERCIAL ARBITRATION •

THE BUSINESSMAN IS REPRESENTATIVE of that view of commercial arbitration which can be described as pragmatic and which considers the capacity for effecting quick resolution of disputes as being the dominant element in and paramount feature of commercial arbitration. The businessman tends to be impatient with the legalistic aspects of the process; and until he steps into his role as an arbitrator, the socially responsible nature of commercial arbitration is of subordinate importance to him.

However, this does not mean to imply that commercial arbitration is broadly accepted or even broadly understood by the business community. On the contrary, the very opposite is true. At this point, we are simply attempting to begin with the presumption that commercial arbitration embodies an important business-oriented quality.

THE NATURE OF BUSINESS DISPUTES

The nature of business disputes is not easily defined. The infinite variety of business endeavors and transactions tends to inhibit the development of accurate generalizations concerning business as a whole. However, three general characteristics of business disputes can be identified.

GENERAL CHARACTERISTICS

1. Business disputes occur infrequently. When contrasted to the astronomical number of contacts and transactions which occur among and between businessmen annually, the incidence of disagreements which reach the proportions of outright disputes is microscopic. Although it would be statistically impossible to prove this point (that is, to compare the number of disputes with the number of instances possessing dispute-producing potential), some data on the subject is available. For example,

of 1,673 trade associations sampled by the authors, only 71 reported the existence of disputes necessitating recourse to arbitration for resolution; of those, the largest annual number of disputes in any one association was 20. Of course, as has been written earlier, many disputes are settled before reaching arbitration, and other disputes are brought to litigation. This does not invalidate the point that with reference to almost any standard the number is extremely small. There are, however, exceptions to this generalization. In certain industries, particularly soft goods and commodities (these have been excluded from the above cited survey), frequent disputes, mainly over quality, are a recognized and accepted fact of life. In such industries, smoothly functioning machinery has been developed internally to cope with these disputes.

2. Business disputes are influenced by the differing amounts of economic power possessed by the parties to the disputes. Participation in a business dispute drains off two critical resources—time and money—which normally would be employed in the day-to-day operations of a business. A large corporation with a self-contained legal department can usually absorb such dilution of effort far more easily than a small business. In addition a small seller often considers it unhealthy to challenge a large continuing buyer on a given transaction. For example, a manufacturer of transistors might sell 50 percent of his output on a continuing basis to a large computer manufacturer. Even if the computer manufacturer were to reject arbitrarily a given shipment for what might be termed debatable or capricious reasons, it is unlikely that the transistor manufacturer would argue the point too actively. However, large-scale economic power is not an unmixed blessing. In recent years, the Government has carefully scrutinized the so-called oligopolistic tendencies of big business, and the large corporation has become increasingly concerned with its image as a good citizen. Such concern has, to some extent, neutralized its ability and reduced its desire to employ economic leverage in the settlement of business disputes.

" 'Every man for himself,' said the elephant as he danced among the chickens, may well have described the attitude and outlook of big business in the days of Rockefeller and Carnegie and railroad robber barons. But nowadays many really big corporations are not eager to dance among the chickens; the consequences are or may be too unpleasant."[1]

3. The businessman does not as a rule attach great importance to winning or losing a particular business dispute. This is the most difficult

---

[1] Raymond A. Bauer, Ithiel de Sola Pool, Lewis Anthony Dexter, *American Business and Public Policy* (New York: Atherton Press, 1963), p. 266.

characteristic to substantiate because there are obviously occasions when a particular dispute can mean survival or bankruptcy for a businessman. But when considered against the broad range of business transactions, a single dispute is usually not as important as a continuing business relationship or a corporate image (as suggested above). "In the law the rendering of exact justice in the matter presented is a final aim. But in business the settlement of a given dispute is not the most important thing. The big thing is the relationship between the parties. In its formal tribunals the law must ignore this preservation of relations between the parties, however momentous."[2]

Even when there exists no concern for a continuing relationship, disputes are carefully avoided. There are always a few businessmen who seem to relish a dispute, but most are not disputatious by nature and become committed to a fight only when they see themselves seriously threatened. This peaceful outlook is not the product of any special amiability peculiar to businessmen but rather of an awareness that, by and large, disputes are dysfunctional for business. As one electronics executive put it, "Business disputes are noise in the circuit of business operations. The best thing to do is to dispose of them quickly in order to clear the circuit for more efficient and effective operations." A former managing editor of the *Harvard Business Review* said, ". . . to a businessman especially, time is money, and the vexatious delays in litigation, the interruptions to business caused by recurrent consultations and legal hearings, and the mental disruptions accompanying controversies of this sort are all inimical to the proper formulation of business policies and the efficacious pursuit of business activities."[3]

ALTERNATIVE METHODS OF SETTLEMENT

Unfortunately, disputes continue to arise; and when they are unavoidable, the businessman should select the appropriate dispute-settling method from among several alternatives. We will discuss four alternatives: capitulation, litigation, negotiation, and commercial arbitration.

Capitulation. There are occasions when it appears appropriate to

[2] Jerome L. Abrams, "Arbitration, Courts and Corporate Problems: A Semantic Approach," *The Arbitration Journal,* Vol. 9, No. 3 (1954), p. 124. (Quoting Herbert Harley, Secretary of the American Judicature Society.)
[3] Carl F. Taeusch, "Extrajudicial Settlement of Controversies, The Businessman's Opinion: Trial at Law. v. Nonjudicial Settlement," *University of Pennsylvania Law Review,* Vol. 83, No. 2 (December 1934), p. 4.

extinguish a dispute before it actually becomes apparent. The situation of the transistor manufacturer described above is a case in point. Taeusch comments:

> . . . of grave import to the businessman is the possible loss of good will through the development of a reputation for resorting to legal methods of settlement. As a result of such undesirable effects, even of successful litigation, businessmen have frequently become notoriously "soft"—in connection with collecting accounts, accepting returned goods, allowing unearned discounts, or permitting bank overdrafts—rather than assert even the minimum of legal or moral rights which are essential to a sound political-economic society.[4]

However, a policy of capitulation can eventually result in serious problems, much in the same way that a labor relations policy of "peace at any price"[5] can eventually run costs up to an unacceptable level. A business that gains the dubious reputation of being a patsy soon finds itself in a very tenuous competitive position.

Litigation. A study of arbitration is necessarily rooted in the arbitration literature, and this literature, almost imperceptibly but inexorably, tends to convince the reader that there is little need for litigation in commercial disputes. Such an assertion, however, denies the vast historical body of commercial law, the extensive commercial practice of thousands of attorneys, and the opinions of such noted educators as Dean Roscoe Pound of the Harvard Law School, who said:

> In matters of property and commercial law, where the economic forms of the social interest in the general security—security of acquisitions and security of transaction—are controlling, mechanical application of fixed, detailed rules or of rigid deductions from fixed conceptions is a wise social engineering. Our economically organized society postulates certainty and predictability as to the incidents and consequences of industrial undertakings and commercial transactions extending over long periods. Individualization of application and standards that regard the individual circumstances of each case are out of place here. . . . Mechanical application of rules as a mere repetition precludes the tendency to individualization which would threaten the security of acquisitions and the security of transactions.[6]

Adherents of commercial arbitration and of the arbitration philosophy in general seem consistently to make the error of denying the efficiency

[4] *Ibid.,* p. 5.
[5] S. H. Slichter, J. J. Healy, E. R. Livernash, *The Impact of Collective Bargaining on Management* (Washington, D. C.: The Brookings Institution, 1960), p. 811.
[6] From Dean Pound's *Interpretations of Legal History,* p. 154, as quoted by Judge Stanley Mosk, "Arbitration versus Litigation," *The Arbitration Journal,* Vol. VII, No. 4 (1952), p. 226.

and appropriateness of the courts in certain disputes. This denial does not usually take the form of an affirmative declaration. As one very informed commentator observes, "No responsible supporter of arbitration would ever say that it should replace litigation, or that it is a panacea." The denial is, however, inherent in the fact that conspicuously absent from the arbitration literature is any discussion of the constraints and limitations of arbitration. The implications are that there are none. Chapter IV will explore this point further.

Critics of commercial arbitration (in almost every case attorneys, law school professors, or members of the judiciary) often have compounded the problems involved in examining the process objectively. Their criticism either focuses on a refutation of the advantages claimed for arbitration or consists of an unfavorable comparison of the mechanics of arbitration with the mechanics of litigation. The refutation is accomplished by citing specific cases in which the advantages did not occur, and the comparison reveals that safeguards which exist in litigation are not present in arbitration. It is very seldom that the criticism adopts the viewpoint of the businessman or attempts to isolate those kinds of disputes which are particularly amenable to arbitration and those which are more properly litigated.

While not expressing a businessman's viewpoint, the following list represents one attempt to catalog some of the dispute situations which are more appropriate to litigation than arbitration:[7]

1. Cases involving difficult questions of law or fact where pretrial procedures are likely to be of substantial assistance.

2. Cases where a decision according to law is wanted both on the procedural level and on the merits level.

3. Cases where a jury trial is wanted.

4. Cases where the expense of arbitration substantially exceeds the expense of court hearing, without compensating advantages.

5. Cases where appellate review of the applicable legal principle is desired.

6. Cases in which special knowledge of arbitration is not essential to obtaining a correct or equitable result.

7. Cases where proper procedural safeguards cannot be obtained by agreement with respect to (a) the personnel of arbitrators; (b) the right to rely on law and rules of evidence or modification thereof; (c) the right

---

[7] "Some Observations on Commercial Arbitration" by Charles Horowitz of the Seattle Bar, September 1961.

to use pretrial techniques; (d) the right to proper hearing dates with respect to the hearing itself and the constituent parts thereof; (e) the right to a decision in which the arbitrators make findings and give their reasons.

It must be remembered that this list has been developed by an attorney operating within a legal frame of reference. The latter sections of this chapter will describe situations in which commercial arbitration has been used successfully. A knowledge of these situations may assist the businessman in arriving at a policy toward dispute settlement by litigation which recognizes the seven cautions of Horowitz above, but, at the same time, is tempered by an evaluation of the usefulness of commercial arbitration.

Negotiation. Our research indicates that, generally, businessmen prefer to settle their differences by negotiation rather than by other means. The general counsel of the Bulova Watch Company states, "Fortunately, our disputes which are not resolved by negotiations between parties are infrequent." The vice president of a large corporation manufacturing a well-known soft drink says, "We are perhaps fortunate in that only rarely do we seem to have disputes of such a character that an adjudication thereof by a third party, either judicially or by arbitration, is called for." This type of response is repeated frequently. Disputes do not occur often, and when they do they are not usually of such a nature as to require third-party adjudication. The use of negotiation to settle business disputes is somewhat akin to collective bargaining between management and labor. When a third party is required for settlement— in the labor/management case, it would take the form of compulsory arbitration—the parties know that they and the process have both failed. Similarly, when businessmen reach the point where they must bring their dispute to a third party, there is in all likelihood a little of that same sense of failure.

Despite the preference for settling disputes by negotiation, this is sometimes not practical, feasible, or equitable. There are disputes for which a mutually satisfactory solution cannot be hammered out by the parties. In the privacy of negotiation, different levels of economic power can again become disproportionately significant. Occasionally, the negotiation process takes more time than it is worth.

Finally, as was indicated in the discussion of trade associations, the propensity to negotiate seems to develop and flourish where there exists a smoothly functioning third-party dispute-settling mechanism.

Commercial arbitration. The process has been described in some detail in Chapter I. The relative advantages and disadvantages for the businessman will be discussed later in this chapter.

WHO SELECTS THE METHOD OF SETTLEMENT?

A business dispute is not a separate phenomenon external to the day-to-day operations of a business. It is, rather, a fact of business life which frequently requires the assistance and advice of a particular specialist, the attorney. The relationship of this specialist to a business dispute is no different from the relationship of an engineer to a technical problem, an industrial relations expert to a labor problem, or a banker to a financial problem. In all cases, the general manager seeks special advice but reserves the prerogative of making the final decision. The particular competence of the specialist does not exempt the general manager from the decision-making process.

In the case of dispute settlement, there is evidence to indicate that the general manager does not intend to be exempted from this decision. A group of 25 top management executives, attending the Advanced Management Program at the Harvard Business School, were asked: "Who in the company should make the decisions concerning business disputes? General manager only? Legal counsel only? General manager and legal counsel, with counsel controlling? General manager and legal counsel, with general manager controlling? Other?" Twenty-one independently answered that such decisions should be made by the general manager and legal counsel, with general manager controlling.

But this does not appear to be the way it works in practice. As noted later, a vast majority of businessmen appear to be unfamiliar with, confused about, or apathetic toward commercial arbitration. On the other hand, a survey of inside corporation counsels indicates the possession of at least a working knowledge of commercial arbitration by at least 90 percent of the respondents. It might be hypothesized that counsel is making all the decisions concerning the use of commercial arbitration.

It is understandable that the businessman would have no objection to this as long as he believed that commercial arbitration could be of no use to him in solving business disputes. But if he accepts the premise that there are disputes which are particularly appropriate for and susceptible to commercial arbitration, it follows that he should not want to leave decisions concerning its use entirely in the hands of counsel.

Although, as Chapter IV will indicate, many attorneys recommend the use of commercial arbitration, the antipathy of some attorneys has already been suggested. At least two large corporations encountered in our research are firmly opposed to the inclusion of any arbitration provisions in their contracts. We suspect there are quite a few more. Since our research has uncovered no logical reason why arbitration should be considered totally inapplicable and therefore to be avoided completely, we can only surmise that such prohibitions are established by counsels hostile to the process. We will examine the nature of legal hostility in Chapter IV. For the moment, we only suggest that *the businessman might see advantages from his frame of reference that the hostile lawyer does not see from his;* therefore, it might prove profitable for the businessman to participate in considerations of the use of commercial arbitration in the settlement of business disputes.

THE BUSINESS COMMUNITY AND COMMERCIAL ARBITRATION

A series of interviews with randomly chosen business executives, held in Boston, Houston, New York, Atlanta, Los Angeles, Detroit, San Francisco, Cleveland, and Palm Beach during the period December 1964 and January 1965, suggested that most businessmen were unfamiliar with commercial arbitration. Many immediately confused it with labor arbitration. Others indicated some recognition of the term, but not much interest in it.

GENERAL KNOWLEDGE AND ATTITUDES

In order to test the presumption that businessmen are generally unfamiliar with commercial arbitration, a random sampling of 500 corporation presidents was conducted by the authors. Replies representing a 35 percent response, 173 in all, were received, and the following percentages are developed from this base. In response to the question, "Have you heard of commercial arbitration (not to be confused with labor arbitration)?" 82 percent answered that they either had little knowledge of commercial arbitration or had never heard of it. Making up the remaining 18 percent, 11 percent indicated that they were familiar with it and an additional 7 percent declared that they had participated in an arbitration.

The accompanying table shows, by industry, the varying degrees of familiarity with commercial arbitration. Although the sample used was not large, there is an indication that the impression gained from our interviews was correct and that only approximately one businessman in five has a working knowledge of commercial arbitration. Additionally, it is not surprising to find a large proportion of those familiar with commer-

DEGREES OF FAMILIARITY WITH COMMERCIAL ARBITRATION

*Little**		*Familiar**		*Participant**	
Industrial tools	4	Textiles	2	Construction supplies	1
Construction	2	Transportation	1	Forging & castings	3
Food	1	Electrical equip.	3	Bank	1
Investment co.	2	Food	2	Textiles	4
Bank	4	Insurance	1	Electrical comp.	1
Industrial Equip.	5	Petroleum	2	Insurance	1
Textiles	4	Real Estate	1	Education equip.	1
Wholesaler	1	Industrial equip.	2		
Publisher	2	Livestock	1		
Rubber products	1	Coal	1		
Paper	2	Construction	2		
Mechanical sub-assemblies	2	Publishing	2		
Castings	2				
Electronic parts	1				

* Numbers indicate frequency of response on an increasing scale of 1 through 5.

cial arbitration to be concentrated within the textile and construction industries, as these industries have historically employed commercial arbitration to settle disputes.

Occasionally, we encountered a specific dislike of commercial arbitration on the part of the businessman. Such a reaction might be a transference of a dislike for the institution of labor arbitration. Many businessmen believe that labor arbitration is gradually eroding the prerogatives formerly reserved for management and therefore should be resisted strenuously. This animosity, however, usually took the form of a tirade against compromise. Commercial arbitration was seen as being synonymous with compromise by the critical businessmen with whom we were speaking. The Secretary of one corporation said, ". . . it has been our experience that the result tends to be a 'middle-of-the-road' approach rather than a clean-cut decision . . . if I had to make a choice I would rather gamble with a court trial and attendant costs rather than risk a final determination by an individual or a panel whose outlook is compromise. . . ."

THE MEANINGS OF COMPROMISE

Throughout our research effort we have found that many participants in the arbitration process have had difficulty with the concept of compromise. It is a word which means different things to different people.

Some people consider it an expression of highly civilized conduct; others see it as an abandonment of principle. In arbitration, too, the word is employed to describe two very different kinds of decisions. We have termed one form of arbitral compromise as *honorific compromise*. This occurs when, for example, two firms are in dispute over the value of certain material and the arbitrator, after careful examination of quality, damage, and other factors, applies his expertise and assesses a value somewhere between the two claims. The valuation decision is not related to the claims of the parties except to the extent that, as is characteristic of claims and counterclaims, they describe the outer parameters of the dispute. The arbitrator is using his own innate sense of what is fair, rather than attempting to find a solution that will satisfy both of the contending parties. Such compromise is a proper and respectable function of commercial arbitration.

However, there is another form of arbitral compromise, which we have called *invidious compromise*. This occurs when the arbitrator conceives himself as having a license to "split the difference" between the parties even though such a decision bears no relation to the facts of the case. Unfortunately, this route seems to be taken occasionally by the arbitrator who finds it too difficult to pound out a solution based on the application of his special competence to the facts and employs this kind of compromise in order to escape from this responsibility. These occasional instances of invidious compromise draw criticism and make the entire process of commercial arbitration suspect in the eyes of certain businessmen. There is also a tendency for some people to regard as invidious what is actually honorific.

DELEGATION TO COUNSEL

Previously, we indicated that the desire to retain control and the possibility of economic advantage should motivate the businessman to participate with his attorney in the decision to use or not to use commercial arbitration. In practice, not one businessman interviewed (with the exception of those interviewed in connection with trade associations) was ready to become involved in a commercial arbitration proceeding without the assistance of counsel. As will be discussed in detail in Chapter IV, the influence of the lawyer upon the businessman in this matter is critical. General Georges F. Doriot, president of American Research and Development Corporation, puts it this way: "You can't blame the businessman for deferring to the lawyer. If something of a legal nature goes wrong, he must be able to hold the lawyer responsible."

While in theory the businessman proposes to retain control over all decisions, in practice he occasionally delegates portions of that control. The future of commercial arbitration depends to a very great extent on the degree to which the businessman feels motivated to reassert his interest in the arbitration process and to share its sponsorship with the attorney.

DOLLARS AND SENSE IN BUSINESS DISPUTES

One of the methods occasionally employed by businessmen in order to measure their own performance in a given area is to find out what is being done by other businessmen in similar area. By observing the relative degree of success achieved by others with a particular mechanism or program, a businessman is better able to make a judgment concerning the applicability of such a mechanism or program to his own operations. An idea or an approach can exist in obscurity until suddenly it is put to use in a new and innovative fashion and thereafter is adopted universally. For example, the critical path method antedated the Polaris program. But the brilliant use of this method in controlling the development of Polaris made PERT a household word throughout industry. As Victor Hugo once said, nothing is so powerful as an idea whose time has come.

USER ATTITUDES

In recognition of this, we attempted to obtain some idea of the economic usefulness of commercial arbitration by surveying 304 businessmen who had participated in American Arbitration Association supervised arbitration proceedings and obtaining their attitudes toward certain aspects of commercial arbitration. We received 96 responses to our survey, and all following percentages are based upon this figure. Of those responding, 74 percent considered themselves to have been winners of the arbitration proceeding. However, not all the losers were displeased. Eighty-five percent of the total responding reported that the trend in their company was toward the use of commercial arbitration. One of the "loser" respondents stated: ". . . one arbitration, even though we lost, was handled well and we felt it was fair. One arbitration due to lack of understanding of the problem by the arbitrator had the award split three ways, and was no real honest answer to the problem." Another "loser" said, "We have had only one experience with commercial arbitration and . . . our experience in this instance was not too good and we blame ourselves by not having full knowledge of the arbitrator—who incidentally [is] an honest man but not experienced in and understanding of the problems involved. We will, if need be, try it again because we believe it has a very useful purpose and can be a quick and cheap way to settle business differences." It is significant that in both cases displeasure focused upon the arbitrator and in both cases the parties were willing to try again.

The principal criterion for deciding whether to use arbitration was the nature of the matter in dispute. Of the respondents, 57 percent stated that they chose arbitration when the dispute was mainly over facts. Other reasons listed included speed of resolution, cost of procedure, need for technical expertise, desirability of privacy, and dollar value of amount in dispute. Commercial arbitration was used wherever possible by 64 percent of the respondents, and 50 percent reported that their policy toward commercial arbitration was based on past experience.

In response to the question "What is your general preference between court litigation and commercial arbitration?" 75 percent preferred commercial arbitration, 20 percent preferred litigation, and the remainder had no preference.

We recognize that this information is drawn from a very small sample. However, it still indicates a relatively high degree of satisfaction with the commercial arbitration procedure. What is there about commercial arbitration which makes these businessmen react so positively?

One respondent commented: "The arbitration provision was inserted by counsel in agreements dealing with the construction of a building to be acquired by the corporation. Purposes: to have relatively speedy determination without excessive bitterness utilizing the expertise of the arbitrator in a specialized field." This statement covers most of the supposed advantages of commercial arbitration as seen by the businessman. The questionnaire tested the attitudes of businessmen toward several of these advantages. Of the respondents, 86 percent considered expense a positive aspect of commercial arbitration, 6 percent considered it a negative aspect, and 8 percent had no opinion. Speed was a positive aspect to 90 percent, 1 percent thought it to be negative, and 9 percent had no opinion. Informality was a positive aspect to 84 percent, 7 percent thought it negative, and 9 percent had no opinion. Only 6 percent considered maintenance of goodwill to be a positive aspect. This can be related to the earlier conjecture that negotiation rather than a third-party proceeding is the method to be employed if the principal goal is the maintenance of goodwill. Five percent considered this to be a negative aspect, and 29 percent had no opinion. Equity of award was a positive aspect to 72 percent of respondents, 7 percent considered it a negative aspect, and 21 percent had no opinion. Finally, competence of arbitrators was considered to be a positive aspect by 69 percent of the respondents, negative by 8 percent, and 23 percent had no opinion. The attitudes toward the aspects of speed of resolution, expense or cost, and informality of procedure indicate that those aspects were considered to be the more significant attributes of commercial arbitration according to the businessman.

THE ATTRIBUTES

1. *Speed of resolution.* Early in 1964, *Time* carried an article entitled "Contracts," which read in part:

> As every businessman knows, litigation of commercial quarrels can be agonizingly slow and annoyingly expensive. In many U.S. cities it takes months or years to bring a suit to trial; beyond that lie the delays of appeal. Meanwhile, costs pile up and claims remain unpaid. There is many a program for speeding up justice, but reform, too, moves slowly, if at all. Faced with delay and frustration in the courts, more and more U.S. firms are using arbitration as a means of resolving disputes. Even for the loser it saves time and money. . . .[8]

It is virtually impossible to compare how long it takes to resolve a given dispute by litigation and by commercial arbitration.[9] The same case is never presented to both courtroom and tribunal. All available evidence, however, indicates that commercial arbitration is considerably faster.

A few years ago, a large chemical concern had a license to manufacture one of the sulpha drugs under a patent granted to another drug company. Subsequently, the chemical firm secured a patent for a specific formula and thereupon claimed it no longer had to pay royalties to the drug company. Under an arbitration clause in the license agreement, the drug company demanded arbitration of the dispute and claimed accumulated royalties for close to $4 million.

Both parties were represented by nationally known law firms, and at a conference they agreed that the arbitrators should include a chemical engineer familiar with organic chemistry and patent law problems, a dis-

[8] *Time*, February 14, 1964, p. 75.
[9] However, Mr. Louis Lauer, Director of the Columbia Project for Effective Justice, Columbia University, is attempting to simulate such a comparison in the course of his research into the arbitration of accident claims.

tinguished lawyer, and an accountant in case questions should arise concerning accounting under the contract.

Association panels were screened and a list consisting of chemical engineers, accountants, and lawyers was sent to the parties. Both agreed upon a prominent New York accountant, organic chemist, and patent lawyer as their first choices. The lawyer selected was counsel for one of the country's largest manufacturers, and the accountant was a former president of the New York State Society of Certified Public Accountants.

Since counsel for both parties feared that information presented in litigation might be used by outside parties, they welcomed the privacy of the arbitration hearings. The matter was resolved after two days' hearings, and the drug concern was awarded approximately $1,750,000. We can only speculate on the length of time it would have taken to process this dispute through litigation.

Not all commentators on commercial arbitration are convinced that the process offers the speed of resolution claimed for it. One attorney says, "Are arbitrations speedier than court proceedings? I doubt it."[10] He proceeds to describe arbitration cases in which one party attempts to delay by questioning arbitrability and applicability of clause and by using dilatory tactics to stretch out the proceedings. He suggests that the alleged tendency of the arbitrator to hear all evidence further lengthens the proceedings and that the absence of pretrial proceedings tends to transform the arbitration hearings into discovery sessions. Cases are cited to illustrate each of these criticisms.

A study of arbitration at the American Arbitration Association conducted under the auspices of the University of Chicago in 1956 reported the following: "Typically the cases in the sample [545] were disposed of in 60 to 90 days. Of the cases, 57 percent were either withdrawn or went to final award in less than 90 days from filing. . . . Of the cases which were not interrupted between hearings for more than 14 days, 77 percent were disposed of in less than 90 days."[11]

Our findings, derived from a much narrower statistical base, indicate that in commercial arbitration under the American Arbitration Association, the average time between filing and final award is still about three months. Both studies indicate that trade association arbitration is generally even faster. The average case in commercial litigation takes approximately

[10] Edward N. Costikyan, "Notes and Views," *New York Law Journal,* February 27, 1964, p. 1.
[11] Hal M. Smith, "Commercial Arbitration at the American Arbitration Association, *The Arbitration Journal,* Vol. II, No. 1 (1956), p. 17.

14 months. (See Chapter V for a more detailed discussion of this comparison.) Therefore, it does not seem that the criticism cited two paragraphs ago is particularly valid.

Both litigation and arbitration are susceptible to delaying tactics on the part of the parties. However, our interviews with a large number of businessmen lead us to conclude that businessmen see little value in delay with regard to business disputes. The level of satisfaction with commercial arbitration apparent from the response to the questionnaire argues that businessmen see value in the speed of the commercial arbitration process.

2. Expense or cost of resolution. Most businessmen are familiar with return-on-investment or payback calculations. Alternative investments are analyzed and choices between them are made on the basis of comparative economic advantage. This approach is applicable to choices among methods for the settlement of business disputes.

The case for economy through arbitration is succinctly stated in a pamphlet published by the New York Chamber of Commerce in May 1952.[12] It says in part:

> The cost of arbitration is reasonable, because among other things there is no undue expenditure of a lawyer's time in procedural formalities on preparation for a technical trial, but a very economic use of his time when it is required in the preparation and presentation of the merits. Neither is there disruption of the parties' and the witnesses' business in preparation for and during the trial.
>
> While docket fees aren't high, court suits generally require expensive daily transcripts of the testimony. The fees of "expert witnesses" and lawyers may run into a large expenditure of money. If the jury disagrees the whole expense has to be undertaken again. Many times the small businessman would rather drop his claim than get involved in lengthy litigation. In arbitration, transcripts aren't usually necessary . . . principals and witnesses are not held for days in court and away from their work . . . lawyers' fees are incurred for a shorter period of time . . . a case is heard just once.

The American Arbitration Association offers the following example of savings through arbitration.[13] The New Village Realty Corporation was about to announce plans for branching out from low-cost home building into large-scale cooperative apartment-house construction when a group of home owners, alleging faulty workmanship in their suburban develop-

---

[12] Chamber of Commerce of the State of New York, "Let's Arbitrate" (New York: by the Chamber of Commerce, May 1962).
[13] American Arbitration Association, *Ask Any Fair-minded Man* (New York: by the Association).

ment, began suit for $100,000. The timing was most unfortunate, for while the corporation was confident it could defend itself successfully in the long run, tying up that much money would delay the project and perhaps kill it. A quick settlement was urgently needed. Fortunately, the home owners were equally interested in speed. When arbitration was suggested as an alternative to extensive litigation, they readily accepted.

A few weeks after the case was put in the hands of the American Arbitration Association, both sides sat facing each other in a hearing room. At the head of the table were an architect, a manufacturer of building materials, and an insurance executive experienced in housing problems. All three were impartial arbitrators, selected from the American Arbitration Association's panels by attorneys for both sides.

Although the arbitrators charged no fees, they gave freely of their time. After a few hours of hearings, they visited the development to see for themselves whether the home owners had justifiable grievances. They found that New Village had failed to do some of the work, but the defaults were not nearly as many as were claimed. The award of the arbitrators directed the corporation to finish the job within a time limit or refund some money to the home owners who could then call in other contractors to do the work.

By getting a quick and fair decision, the New Village Realty was able to release tied-up funds and take advantage of the strategic moment for expansion.

Not everyone is convinced concerning the economy inherent in commercial arbitration: "In our experience, by and large, the cost of arbitration has been substantially higher than the cost of a proceeding in court. The reasons are the direct result of the informality of arbitration proceedings and the general tendency of arbitrators to hear every scrap of evidence 'for what it is worth.' The result is to permit arbitration proceedings to be drawn on interminably."[14] The writer then calls attention to postponements, costs of transcripts, excessive filing fees, arbitration fees, and the time spent in the equivalent of discovery proceedings. He concludes his argument by saying that: ". . . the claim that arbitration is economical is not borne out by actual experience if one includes in the cost of arbitration additional cost items which would not be present in a court proceeding."[15]

These criticisms embody a good deal of truth as long as the critic postulates the existence of delay and postponement, the requirement for a

[14] Costikyan, *op. cit.,* p. 1.
[15] *Ibid.*

transcript, and the necessity to pay arbitrators. In the course of our examination of the process, we have found that payment of the arbitrator becomes a factor only when the case is delayed and does stretch out.

While we do not have exact statistics on the frequency and length of delays in arbitration, Professor Smith's figures on speed of resolution indicate that delays are neither endemic nor extensive. Professor Smith comments directly on the subject. After noting that delays incident to the selection of arbitrators and occurring as postponements between hearings occur more frequently in cases in which the parties are represented by attorneys, he states the following:

> Where both parties were represented by attorneys, 43% of the cases were decided in less than 90 days and 21% in less than 60 days. Where neither party brought an attorney, 78% of the cases were decided in less than 90 days and 49% in less than 60 days. The attorneys would seem to be bringing some of their court practices and skills to arbitration.[16]

(In fairness it should be noted that attorneys are usually used in the larger, more complex cases, which understandably take more time.)

When attorneys are not employed, as in trade association arbitration, costs of resolution are negligible. It appears that on the average the process itself facilitates economy, but occasionally participants in or parties to the hearing can, by their actions, inflate the cost. It is also fair to say that certain complex cases brought to arbitration do cost a good deal of money to resolve. However, such cases would be expensive in either courtroom or tribunal. In the final analysis, the question for the businessman must be a determination of the value of the legal safeguards he must trade off to obtain the economy implicit in the speed and finality of commercial arbitration.

3. *Expertise of arbitrators.* The professional competence of the arbitrator is attractive to the businessman because a commercial dispute arises out of an environment that usually possesses its own folkways, mores, and technology. Most businessmen interviewed contended that commercial disputes should be considered within the framework of such an environment. No matter how determinedly judge and lawyer work to acquire an understanding of a given business or industry, they cannot hope to approximate the practical wisdom distilled from 30 or 40 years of experience. Expert witnesses can be and often are confronted by other expert witnesses with conflicting viewpoints. As Taeusch says: "The businessman very definitely has the opinion, indeed the conviction, that the lawyer and the

---

[16] Smith, *op. cit.,* p. 18.

judge are, after all, amateurs in matters of business controversy . . . and frequently the judge has to be painstakingly informed regarding matters which to the litigants appear to be elementary. . . ."[17]

Since the majority of the cases brought to arbitration involve questions of fact rather than questions of law, the expert is able to exercise his particular skill:

> Arbitration appeals to some railroads because it provides an opportunity for them to submit technical disputes to men well versed in the industry's affairs. "We've used it and favor it over the courts because juries just don't know anything about our business contracts," says Joseph H. Wright, General Counsel for the Illinois Central Railroad. In matters of awards particularly, juries too often judge on the basis of "emotion and feeling," Mr. Wright declares, adding that experienced railroad men are better equipped to handle complex inter-railroad disputes and are less inclined to make what he calls "unreasonable" awards.[18]

Critics of arbitration claim that the arbitrator is generally not as adept at the art of judging as is the professional judge. This question will be discussed in Chapter III. Others imply that the arbitrator is presumptuous when he assumes the posture of a judge. This attitude will be discussed in Chapter IV. It is significant that neither of these criticisms concern the question which would be of greatest importance to the businessman—Is the arbitrator efficient and effective? Our interview evidence and the level of satisfaction displayed in the responses to the questionnaires indicate that he is. In the words of the late Judge Learned Hand, "In trade disputes one of the chief advantages of arbitration is that the arbitrators can be chosen who are familiar with the practices and customs of the calling. . . ."[19]

4. *Continuity of relationship.* The existence of a long history of successful trade-association arbitration is a testimonial to the efficacy of the process in maintaining the continuity of a reasonably smooth relationship. In commodity transactions, the maintenance of buyer-seller rapport is imperative, and yet disputes over quality and valuation are bound to occur. Since the relationship between the parties is almost inescapable, capitulation is not a viable alternative. Litigation would be far too costly, and the contentious atmosphere of the courtroom would tend to rupture communications between the parties. Negotiation would work in some cases, but in a trade where disputes occurred frequently, even this method

---

[17] Taeusch, *op. cit.,* p. 4.
[18] *Wall Street Journal,* May 23, 1961, p. 1.
[19] As quoted in "How to Settle Business Disputes Painlessly," *Business Management,* Vol. 21, No. 2 (November 1961), p. 60.

would consume too much time. Commercial arbitration serves the purpose very well. For example the Rubber Trade Association (New York) arbitrates nearly 1,000 quality determinations, and the New England Cotton Buyers (Boston) arbitrates the quality of more than 25,000 bales of cotton each year.

Itek, a manufacturer of electro-optical systems, employs commercial arbitration in order to sustain a relationship (and a concomitant inflow of components) with its suppliers during the resolution of any dispute which arises under the contract. The arbitration clause specifies that pending final determination, the parties shall proceed diligently with the performance of the contract.

One equipment leasing firm said that disputes arising under leases which require the lessee to provide services are particularly suitable for arbitration.

One writer reports that: "A manufacturer of large transportation units suggested the use of arbitration clauses in warranty clauses. . . . Good customer relationships might be better presented in arbitration than in litigation."[20]

Of course, a great many disputes occur between parties who have little or no interest in continuing their relationship. For these people, this particular attribute of commercial arbitration has little value.

5. *Privacy.* There are a number of kinds of disputes which might prove embarrassing or costly to the parties if the circumstances were to become public knowledge.

For example, a large rubber company recently encountered a situation in which one of its employees attempted to gain employment with a competitor. The rubber company, fearing disclosure of important technical secrets, brought legal action to prevent this employee from disclosing such secrets. However, in order to win its case, the rubber company had to prove it possessed such secrets by disclosing them to the court. The incorporation of an arbitration clause in the original employment contract would have provided a confidential forum for the settlement of this particular dispute.

Business reputation can suffer immeasurably from the public airing of a dispute. Occasionally, the very existence of a dispute can cause damage far out of proportion to the actual circumstances. A case from the files of the American Arbitration Association can illustrate this point. In a

---

[20] Robert Coulson, "Tailoring Arbitration to Business Needs," 19 *Business Lawyer* 925 (1964).

case occurring not long ago, a large refinery discovered that the foundations and sections of a wall of a building were cracked. The contractor was obliged, at considerable expense, to rectify the condition. Eventually, the contractor demanded arbitration of a cement supply company, claiming that the original cement was inferior and not up to specifications. Upon receipt of the demand for arbitration, within 48 hours the Association sent both parties a list consisting of experts in quality of cement, foundation work, and general contracting. Within two weeks a hearing was held, a few days later the actual foundation and walls were examined, and shortly thereafter an award was made denying the claim of the contractor on the grounds that the errors had occurred because of improper handling and hurried workmanship on the part of the contractor.

The privacy of the proceedings was worth more than winning the award to the cement company. Even though its product had been upheld as perfect in content, the company could have suffered badly if a long damage suit were tried in the courts and if the public had read only one side of the story. In addition, the building was done in an area where millions of dollars worth of contracts for cement work were annually let by the state government. Privacy also prevented the problem from becoming a subject for political accusations.

In still another case, a nationally known manufacturer had to withdraw a commodity from the market on complaints that a particular product caused skin eruptions. The manufacturer accused a supplier of shipping faulty material and was accused in turn of faulty processing. Appropriate damage was awarded. Again in this instance, the privacy of the arbitration was maintained and no adverse publicity hurt either party.

Once again, critics contend that a recalcitrant party can vitiate this advantage if he so desires. Other critics contend that the privacy of the tribunal can be misused, that threat of public exposure is occasionally an excellent weapon in a controversy, and that its use should not be gratuitously forfeited.

As before, we agree that these criticisms can be valid for certain specific cases. But, in general, the businessman finds this kind of privacy much to be desired. As one corporation executive said, "None of us sees any value in airing our dirty underwear in public. This is why we seek to negotiate whenever a dispute arises. But when negotiations break down or become impractical, this is why we choose commercial arbitration."

6. *Informality of proceedings.* This advantage was rated highly by the respondents to our questionnaires, and it is difficult to determine the precise motivation for this reaction. It is likely that some businessmen see a rela-

tionship between informality and speed. The arbitration tribunal is informal because it eschews the time-consuming procedural aspects of litigation. Others see a great advantage in the flexibility inherent in the proceedings. Frequently, the tribunal convenes at the site of a dispute.

In one case, an extremely expensive piece of automated machinery had been installed in a factory but had failed to function according to specifications. The buyer brought the dispute to arbitration, and because the machinery involved was part of a permanent installation, the arbitration was held in the factory. The arbitration panel consisted of an expert on the process involved, an expert on automated machinery, and an attorney. After hearing both sides of the case and observing the machine in operation, the arbitrators decided that the problem was one of operator and maintenance-man competence, not of machine operation. A competent operator was obtained, the machine functioned properly, and both parties went away satisfied.

Finally, there exists a belief that the atmosphere in an arbitration tribunal is less contentious than that of a courtroom, both as a result of the simplicity of the procedure and the feeling experienced by a disputing businessman that he is at least among his own. Our interviews with trade association officials substantiate this belief. However, as the procedure of the arbitration tribunal becomes more legalistic in nature, flexibility decreases and the businessman finds the proceedings less identifiable with his normal environment.

Chapter IV will discuss the relationship of legalism and arbitration. It is important for the businessman to be able to determine how much in the way of flexibility he is willing to sacrifice in order to obtain the consistency of judgment which Dean Pound finds so important in the resolution of commercial disputes. As Diesing says in his fine treatise, *Reason in Society:*

> The selective process producing legalism operates apart from any conscious plan or intent of the parties involved. Conscious attention is ordinarily focused on the immediate situation, and people's energies are devoted to getting what they want, protecting what they have, avoiding trouble, preventing others from taking advantage of them. As a result of these varied efforts, some rules and principles get established and clarified while others are rejected and a trend occurs. . . . For instance the trend to rigidity and reliance on precedent is accelerated by mediators anxious to find the most reliable grounds of settlement. . . . They apply the rules directly to a dispute if possible, or, if the rules are not immediately applicable, they make them applicable by appropriate interpretations, clarifications, deductions, or analogies. In so doing they contribute further to the authority

of established principle, and circumscribe further the area of discretion of later mediators.[21]

7. *Maintenance of goodwill.* As has been stated, this attribute of commercial arbitration was rated rather low on a relative scale of importance by the respondents to our questionnaires. Most business executives with whom we spoke agreed that goodwill was maintained by negotiation and that once a dispute reached arbitration, goodwill was no longer a paramount consideration. There are exceptions to this position, however. As we have seen, when there exists a need for the preservation of a relationship, when the technique of negotiating is inapplicable or has failed, and when the tribunal remains informal and nonlegalistic, commercial arbitration can usually avoid the acrimony which sometimes emerges between adversaries in litigation.

In another portion of this chapter we will discuss some of the potential uses of commercial arbitration which are presently being considered by businessmen and others. One of these potential uses is an interesting variation on the theme of goodwill.

THE CURRENT USES OF COMMERCIAL ARBITRATION

Our examination of user attitudes and of the attributes of commercial arbitration suggests certain applications of the process. Most participants agree that commercial arbitration is most appropriate for the resolution of questions of fact rather than questions of law. It is frequently applied to questions of fact involving quality of merchandise and quality of contract performance when a special competence is required in order to render judgment.

Commercial arbitration is appropriate for disputes among groups which have a relatively static membership and are constrained to continue doing business with one another. This accounts for the success of arbitration in the commodity and trade associations and within institutions such as the New York Stock Exchange.

Commercial arbitration is appropriate for disputes which the parties wish to resolve privately—for example, disputes involving technical secrets or corporate reputations.

Commercial arbitration is appropriate when quick resolution is desired. For example, members of the textile industry reported that if they waited for litigation in disputes with many of their smaller customers, such

[21] Paul Diesing, *Reason in Society* (Urbana: University of Illinois Press, 1962), p. 115.

customers might be no longer in existence when the case went to trial. It appears that the mechanics of the free enterprise system at work in the garment trade encourage the employment of commercial arbitration.

One commentator suggested that commercial arbitration advanced the last possible date for a so-called "eve of trial" settlement and would operate to hurry those strategists who delighted in engaging in this particular form of legal brinkmanship.

Commercial arbitration is appropriate when the expected value of a dispute does not equal the cost of litigation. A calculation of the expected value of a dispute must consider the cost of such intangibles as interruptions to business and loss of goodwill, plus any opportunity costs attributable to capital frozen as a result of the dispute, as well as the actual dollar amount involved. A calculation of the cost of litigation should assign some dollar value to the insurance provided by such legal safeguards as strict rules of evidence and the right of appeal, as well as including the actual costs of fees and services.

Some businessmen establish a strict dollar cutoff under which they use commercial arbitration and above which they choose litigation. A very prominent attorney, speaking before a symposium of the City Bar of New York, responded to the question "When is arbitration a disadvantage?" by saying, in part, "[It is a disadvantage] where the interest involved is substantial in money or rights." However, it is difficult to see the logic of a dollar cutoff unless the above considerations are included in the decision.

Commercial arbitration can serve to ameliorate the circumstances that might lead to a dispute as in the case where the process is employed to establish an original valuation and to assist in other elements of contract making. It is also used to settle the disputes arising over valuation. For example, when Federated Department Stores acquired Filene's in Boston in 1949, holders of 1,681 shares of Filene's stock disputed the valuation placed on that stock by a firm of financial consultants. The dispute was settled in arbitration.

Commercial arbitration has also been used to legitimize the resolution of a dispute. This occurred in the case of two rug dealers who represented two families violently at odds with one another. The two dealers arrived at a satisfactory resolution through negotiation but brought the case to arbitration anyway (quietly communicating the results of their negotiations to the arbitrators) in order to assure their militant families that neither of them had in any way capitulated.

A recent survey of 500 corporations of various sizes and in a number of industries brought forth responses which suggested the following uses:

From Consolidated Electrodynamics Corporation, a division of Bell and Howell:

Patent License Agreements: Quite frequently in highly technical product situations covered by patent licenses, disputes arise concerning whether the licensed patent in fact covers a given product manufactured and sold by the licensee. If an arbitration provision were inserted in the agreement, it might be helpful in assisting the parties to resolve the dispute.

Patent Infringement: Although in situations in which a patentee asserts that another party is infringing his patent rights, the parties generally are not contractually bound to each other in any way; however, the development of skills and arbitration capabilities in the patent infringement area would aid greatly in the resolution of such matters on a voluntary basis. Generally speaking, court calendars are such that patent infringement actions are delayed for protracted periods. Both parties must expend considerable amounts to bring matters to issue in such an action, and during this period the patentee must forego royalties to which he feels entitled, and the defendant must continue to carry on activities under a cloud.

Purchase and Sale of Assets and Business: We have on several occasions, in connection with purchase and sales of assets which involved long-term payouts based on activities of the parties in connection with the business, found that arbitration provisions have been extremely effective in resolving or avoiding disputes. . . .

From a major consumer products producer: "We wonder whether or not [arbitration] has been used in resolving *product claims, trademark infringements,* and *unfair advertising disputes.*"

From E. F. MacDonald Stamp Company: "Most recently I have referred to [arbitration] in an agreement which involved the *selection of accounting methods to determine a settlement variable* in the agreement."

From Kaiser Aluminum and Chemical Corporation: "Our *maritime charters* generally contain an arbitration clause."

From an international oil company: "We should like to work out some firm and agreed procedure for disposing of such claims [involving *workmen's compensation of foreign-based American employees*]."

From Pacific Gas and Electric Company: "We incorporate arbitration provisions in several important categories of our *contracts, such as contracts for the purchase [from producers] of natural gas and contracts for the construction of plant facilities.*"

From International Resistance Company:

In our industry there are three areas in which disputes occasionally arise and which might be suitable for arbitration rather than litigation. These are:

Technical personnel raids by one company against another.

Disputes, particularly with respect to *return of inventory between manufacturers and distributors.*

Disputes of all kinds between manufacturers and their O.E.M. [original equipment manufacturer] *customers.*

From Hewitt-Robins Incorporated: "I have been thinking of the possibility of our company adopting a standard arbitration clause in our *engineered systems contracts.*"

From Diana Stores Corporation: "I do use the [arbitration] clause in all of our *employment contracts* and in all our *construction contracts.*"

From City Stores Company: "We are also providing for arbitration of different contractual arrangements, such as, for example, *executive employment agreements.* We certainly would prefer to handle disputes with our own executives along the arbitration route."

From Braniff Airways: "Perhaps a greater use might be made of arbitration provisions in the many *interline agreements and other relationships between airlines.*"

From IBM: "I am looking into one area of additional use of arbitration, namely in the *collection area* where something more than an arbitrary refusal is involved."

Many other respondents offered suggestions which were variations of the above. Finally, there is the major area of international trade arbitration which will be discussed in detail later.

POTENTIAL USES FOR COMMERCIAL ARBITRATION

There are two forces at work in the environment which will shape the future of commercial arbitration: the new technology and the new responsibility. The new technology embraces the extraordinary technical acceleration which is swiftly making anachronisms out of many of our revered social institutions. The new responsibility is the awareness that new social institutions must be created to replace the old.

1. *The new technology.* Later we will discuss the relationship between the proliferation of the automobile and the congestion in many court calendars. The space and defense industries have spawned conglomerate associations of companies which come together on an ad hoc basis to contribute to infinitely complex space or defense programs. The computer has hastened the development of automation. All these phenomena are facets of the new technology, and arbitration has pertinence for them all.

The use of arbitration *to resolve disputes between governmental prime contractors and government subcontractors* was given an encouraging boost on July 10, 1964. On this date the Armed Services Procurement Regulation Committee approved a change in the wording of regulation 3-903.5 (c) which placed arbitration on an equal basis with judicial determinations and voluntary settlements. These disputes, which complicate the relationships between prime and sub and further complicate the life of the already harassed program manager, can be resolved quickly through arbitration. Although indicating that arbitration is not a complete panacea, several of the respondents to the corporate survey reported that they have employed arbitration successfully in this situation.

Preliminary research into the field of *automatic data-processing contract disputes* discloses a substantial potential for controversy. The basic concern is with contractual performance, but the scale of each transaction is measured in multiples of millions of dollars. What method should be used, for example, to resolve a dispute in which one party alleges lack of performance of an automated chemical plant costing $30-odd million? Litigation over such a question could take years, tying up vast amounts of plant and capital. However, a commercial arbitration clause covering such a potential horizon of disputes would have to be tailor-made to the individual circumstances. There seems to be a significant role for such individualized arbitration in the future.

2. *The new responsibility.* Businessmen have become increasingly conscious of their role in society. Searching questions have been asked about the wisdom of allowing so much power to repose within the huge corporations. From some quarters, there is a ceaseless cry for increased government regulation. One of the successful approaches employed by businessmen in order to ward off the imposition of additional government restraints has been sincere self-regulation. For example, the adoption of the code of good practice by the National Association of Broadcasters forestalled government legislation in the area of television programing. As was suggested by one respondent to the corporate survey, commercial arbitration could be utilized as an impartial agent through which to resolve claims of unfair advertising.

One distiller is contemplating the establishment of a commercial arbitration procedure in order to conclude separation arrangements fairly and resolve other disputes with his distributors. He sees commercial arbitration as "grievance procedure for industry."

IBM, searching for methods for displaying corporate good citizenship, writes:

Another possibility concerns the arbitration either with our suppliers or own customers where there is admittedly no legal liability—the claim is rather for overreaching or unfairness or something short of a cause of action. In such instances there are frequently disputes between the parties as to the actual facts or the customs in the trade, and it would be these issues one might like to see resolved by arbitration.

These represent both elements of and evidence of the new responsibility.

THE GROWTH OF COMMERCIAL ARBITRATION

The use of commercial arbitration will increase at a gradual rate. The vast unfamiliarity of businessmen will not be overcome quickly, despite inventive and energetic efforts on the part of the American Arbitration Association and other agencies. There are, however, indications of a reviving business interest. The following comment was characteristic of a number of letters received from corporations:

> Recently it has been suggested to me, on two different occasions, that a dispute concerning the satisfactory performance of our company's products be submitted to arbitration. I must admit that these suggestions were novel to me and because of the lack of any experience with such types of arbitration, I rejected the suggestions made. I would, however, like to know more about whether this type of thing is being done more frequently in industry. I think it would be a good idea to follow such a procedure if this can be practicably accomplished.

An exchange of information among corporations with similar problems should tend to increase acceptance. A communications utility in the East reported that arbitration was not applicable to their operations, but shortly thereafter a Western communications utility reported that arbitration clauses were incorporated in all their construction contracts. A Boston bank which recently participated as claimant in a construction arbitration commented that it could not conceive of other uses in their operations for the process. Four other banks reported using arbitration in both investment and valuation disputes.

New uses will appear. In recent months both the National Association of Small Business Investment Corporations and at least one Better Business Bureau adopted the use of arbitration. New and innovative uses, such as those described previously, will extend the employment of commercial arbitration.

It is unlikely that an explosive expansion in the domestic use of arbitration—such as that which occurred in labor arbitration during World War II and in accident claims arbitration during the 1950's and 1960's—will be repeated, for business disputes are relatively infrequent and, consequently, arbitration is already being employed in many of the situations to which it is applicable.

There are two areas, however, one speculative and one concrete, in which arbitration may play a significant role—the historic civil rights movement and the great international trade expansion. The similarities between the civil rights movement and the labor movement are striking. American labor moved through a period of bloody conflict and suspicious containment and is only now emerging into an era of accommodation and hopefully constructive cooperation with management. The civil rights movement is now where the labor movement was in the mid-1930's—it has achieved its enabling legislation but the conflict goes on. American business is groping for a means of coming to grips with the social and moral challenge presented by the civil rights movement. The general situation is currently so exacerbated that even speculation over the employment of arbitration seems ludicrous. However, containment will ultimately be achieved and at that time the opposing forces in the movement may cease to rely on direct power confrontations to achieve their aims. At this moment American business might find the arbitration mechanism useful.

More immediate is the rapidly increasing involvement of the American businessman in the international business arena. Real growth in the use of commercial arbitration may occur here. A later chapter will examine this possibility.

IS ARBITRATION POWER?

One articulate and persuasive critic of the arbitration process argues that arbitration represents a form of power that is subject to no external authority, answerable only to itself, capable of imposing itself ambitiously, and thus is to be feared and restrained.[22]

It is true that arbitration can contain a coercive element, particularly for the individual and the small business. In one case a company which specialized in the selling of cosmetics from door to door contracted with sales personnel to work for a stipulated period of time or else reimburse the company for "training" received. The contract contained an arbitration clause, but it is unlikely that the prospective sales person saw anything potentially coercive in it. When the sales person became disenchanted with

---

[22] Heinrich Kronstein, "Arbitration Is Power," *New York University Law Review,* Vol. 38 (June 1963), p. 662.

the neighborhood in which she was assigned to sell or with the quality of the merchandise and decided to terminate, the arbitration clause was invoked and the sales person was required to reimburse the company. This contractual relationship prostituted the idea of arbitration in which two parties mutually agree to arbitrate future disputes. The fact that territories and merchandise might have been orally misrepresented to the sales person had no bearing on the arbitration decision. An even more flagrant misuse of arbitration occurred when a juke box concessionaire used a clause to pressure his clients. The clients had no choice but to accept the clause, for without it they could not get a juke box. The arbitrator had no choice but to follow the terms of the contract which was tightly drawn in the concessionaires' favor. In view of the speed of arbitration and the normal absence of appeal, the concessionaire had an excellent club with which to police his clients.

The police potential of arbitration is seen by Kronstein in terms of the trade-association discipline. He describes the use of such methods as ostracism, exclusion, threat of exposure, and the imposition of fines in order to sustain the power of the internal arbitration mechanism.

> Who in the business community can dare to acquire the reputation of disregarding orders and decrees of "friendly" arbitration—regardless of whether he is a member of a trade association establishing arbitration or a third person doing business with member firms.[23]

The use of arbitration as a collection device is clearly described by one attorney. In an article, he describes the use of arbitration in order to police bad credit risks. The speed of arbitration is employed to remove the bad debt from the books whereas in litigation it might linger for years. The finality of the award avoids the possibility of delay through appeal. A clause which specifies arbitration in a particular location avoids the necessity to work through a corresponding attorney and with depositions. The implication is that the prospective debtor has little choice but to submit to the creditor's carefully constructed policing system if he is to have any chance of receiving credit. The article concludes by saying:

> Arbitration, properly used, eliminates or short-circuits an important element of risk involved in every extension of credit, by providing a method of obtaining a prompt settlement of disputes. Similarly, it eliminates or short-circuits a great source of economic waste by obviating needless litigation. Thus, arbitration can be a stabilizing factor in the credit field and should be utilized to its maximum extent. Use it properly, use it when-

[23] *Ibid.*, p. 676.

ever it becomes necessary and your dividends will accrue in the form of reduced credit losses and a lower cost of collection.[24]

There is nothing illegal about this use of arbitration, and there is nothing unusual about restrictive covenants being attached to a loan. It is the strong inference of unequal economic power being exploited, the use of arbitration not as a facilitating device but as a club, that seems to us to be a perversion of the original intent of the process. To some businessmen this particular use of commercial arbitration might be the most interesting one on the entire list. But we would speculate that the acceptability of arbitration under the law would diminish quickly if arbitration was to be used extensively in this fashion. A credit executive armed with the access to summary action which is inherent in arbitration would be about as equally matched with his potential adversary as a pike in a carp pond. When arbitration is used in this fashion, its voluntary character and its claim of being equally and mutually acceptable to the parties is discarded. This is an example of coercive arbitration which serves to illustrate Kronstein's argument.

Kronstein fears the establishment of an extra-legal system by means of which different national legal systems could be circumvented. Arbitrators could select applicable law taking into account contract terms and trade usages.[25] A U.S. Government official saw this same fear as one of the contributing reasons for the failure of the United States to sign the United Nations Convention of 1958 on the Recognition and Enforcement of Foreign Arbitral Awards. He reported that there existed some feeling that the convention was desired by international "power groups" who desired to establish "cartel discipline."

Kronstein's principal concern seems to be with what he sees as a steady encroachment of the private tribunal, the increasing power of the commercial association, and an enlarging potential for the restraint of trade:

> Arbitration is power, and courts are forbidden to look behind it. The protection of awards against judicial interference and, under that umbrella, of the development of organized arbitration as a rule maker have established "judicial powers" other than those provided by federal and state constitutions. It is not possible to maintain any legally established policy or order in domestic and international trade, whether it is an order of full competition protected by anti-trust legislation or any other type of

---

[24] Jules J. F. Hessen, "Arbitration—The Credit Executive's Ally," *Credit Executive* (October 1950), reprinted in *The Arbitration Journal*, Volume 5, No. 4 (1950), p. 295.

[25] Kronstein, *op. cit.*, p. 667.

economic order provided by law, if courts abdicate their power in favor of private tribunals serving private interests.[26]

It is evident that arbitration can be abused and that the speed and summary character of the process can be put to work by a party who is economically much stronger than his adversaries. Arbitration can be made to coerce, control, and discipline, and it is conceivable that arbitration can be used to constrain due process and circumvent legal systems.

However, these serious considerations do not invalidate the basic right of two businessmen to bind themselves to the decision of a third party. This right was clearly enunciated by Judge Andrews:

> The arbitrator is a judge appointed by the parties; he is by their consent invested with judicial functions in the particular case; he is to determine the right as between the parties in respect to the matter submitted, and all questions of fact or law upon which the right depends are, under a general submission, deemed to be referred to him for decision. The court possesses no general supervisory power over awards and if arbitrators keep within their jurisdiction their award will not be set aside because they have erred in judgment either upon the facts or the law.[27]

If arbitration is power, the franchise for such power has been freely given.

Although methods must be found to insure that such a franchise is never coerced from a party and that arbitration is not exploited as a quasi-legal police power, it remains our contention that private tribunals operating under the aegis of the law can effectively serve the social order.

* * *

Businessmen try to avoid disputes. Victory in a particular controversy is not nearly as important to them as a smooth running operation over the long term. Disputes are uneconomical, divert resources from more profitable investments, disturb relationships, take time.

Therefore, the businessman attempts to settle most disputes as expeditiously as possible—occasionally by capitulation if he is in a weak power position, more often through negotiation. When disputes cannot be negotiated, the businessman must choose between litigation and commercial arbitration.

However, the businessman knows very little about commercial arbitration and usually delegates this decision to counsel. Some attorneys are

---

[26] *Ibid.*, p. 699.
[27] *Fudicar vs. Guardian Mutual Life Insurance Co.* 62 N.Y. 392 (1879).

familiar with commercial arbitration and recommend it. Many, however, are either unfamiliar with or hostile to it, and thus the businessman is automatically deprived of any advantages it might possess.

Businessmen users report a high degree of satisfaction with commercial arbitration and see its principal attributes as speed of resolution, economy, expertise of arbitrators, maintenance of relationship, privacy, informality, and maintenance of goodwill. Critics point out that these are not available in certain cases, but statistically the principal advantages—speed, economy, and expertise—appear to be available more often than not.

A few businessmen report many ways in which commercial arbitration may be used innovatively and with economic advantage. It appears to have applications for the future in both the technological and social spheres of business. For example, it is being used successfully to resolve disputes between defense prime and subcontractors. One corporation envisions its use as a "grievance procedure for industry." There is speculation over its application in the future to civil rights controversies. Perhaps the most significant potential lies in the area of international trade.

Arbitration can be abused and can conceivably operate to circumvent the due-process safeguard of the legal system. At least one critic sees it as a locus of unpoliced power accumulated to be employed in restraint of trade or to enforce cartel discipline.

Commercial arbitration once belonged to the businessman; but now, except for pockets of activity in the trade associations, it has been inherited for better or for worse by the attorney. Clearly, the process has some economic value, and it would pay the businessman to assert his interest in it for this reason alone. But the process is slowly being legalized, and it is becoming something other than it was. (See Chapter IV.)

The businessman will never again be able to obtain the complete hegemony over the process that he once possessed. But it is still possible to achieve an accommodation with the lawyer and thus evolve a cosponsorship which would keep the practical and pragmatic element in arbitration alive and active.

The two principal methods by which a businessman could regain some influence in the future of commercial arbitration are:

1. To ensure that the process receives consideration as a dispute-settling mechanism and to take part in any decision selecting such a mechanism.

2. To participate in the development of a strong corps of arbitrators, for it is on the competence of the arbitrator that commercial arbitration must stand or fall.

CHAPTER III

THE ARBITRATOR •

THE ARBITRATOR IS THE KEY to the effectiveness of the arbitration process. Commercial arbitration is deemed fair or unfair, just or unjust, objective or not objective by the fairness, justice, and objectivity displayed by the arbitrator. Therefore, in order to understand and evaluate the arbitration process, it is important to examine the arbitrator, to look at his background, to learn about his attitudes, and to consider all aspects of his role.

The arbitrator is chosen to be a judge. Although there are commentators who consider that judging is a skill which can be developed only through practice such as that obtainable at the legal bench, at least one judge has a somewhat different view of the relationship of arbitration and judging:

> The judge, at his best, is an arbitrator, a "sound man" who strives to do justice to the parties by exercising a wise discretion with reference to the peculiar circumstances of the case. . . . The bench and the bar usually try to conceal the arbitral function of the judge. . . . But although fear of legal uncertainty leads to this concealment, the arbitral function is the central fact in the administration of justice. The concealment has merely made the labor of judges less effective.[1]

Arbitrators are responsible to the parties, and must arrive at a just and final award. They must avoid compromise in its invidious sense. To do this they must be conscientious, deliberate, fair, and sincere in their efforts.

Interpreted narrowly, the full responsibility of the arbitrator is to the

---

[1] Jerome Frank, *Law and the Modern Mind* (New York: 1936), p. 157, as quoted in Jerome L. Abrams, "Arbitration, Courts and Corporate Problems: A Semantic Approach," *The Arbitration Journal,* Vol. 9, No. 3 (1954).

parties. But the arbitrator is acutely conscious of the broader implications which attend his role as a judge. He is motivated by a feeling of responsibility to the business and/or legal community from which he comes, to the public which he serves, and most importantly, to himself, because he is his own sponsor.

Commercial disputes are often extraordinarily complex, clouded with argument, filled with technical difficulties, and aggravated by irrelevancies; somehow the arbitrator must pick his way through these disputes with competence and accuracy. "They think they are King Solomon," wrote one irate respondent to our questionnaire, and, indeed, on occasion they have to be. The skills and attributes which a successful arbitrator must possess, the breadth of his responsibility, and the complexity of the cases combine to place a formidable demand upon him. In the following pages we will introduce these men and examine their attitudes, backgrounds, experience, and education in an attempt to evaluate how effectively they are performing this difficult task.

ARBITRATOR PROFILE

Of the more than 20,000 commercial arbitrators in this country, over 18,000 are members of the American Arbitration Association's panel of arbitrators. The remaining men serve the many trade and professional associations which use their own arbitration mechanisms. Since the total number of commercial arbitration cases held in the country last year is estimated at between 1,500 and 2,000, only a small percentage of the potential arbitrator participants were asked to serve. These are the men that we will describe in this section.

In attempting to establish an arbitrator profile, we have relied on three sources of information. A survey of the American Arbitration Association's arbitrator files was made, an arbitrator questionnaire was circulated, and interviews with both American Arbitration Association and trade association arbitrators were conducted.

Our study indicates that arbitrators come from a wide range of businesses and professions. The most frequent vocations encountered were: attorneys, textile managers, engineers, architects, construction managers, bankers, accountants, and foreign-trade specialists.

It was obvious that the largest single group was made up of lawyers, and our estimates place this group at about 20 percent of the total. Other groups with more than nominal participation were: textile industry managers (16 percent), engineers (9 percent), and architects and construction contractors (8 percent). Token participation was found in such diverse areas as chemicals, trucking, and wigs and hair goods. It is apparent from this diversity of backgrounds that arbitrators were available from almost any field that might have been required by a particular set of circumstances.

Over 90 percent of the arbitrators surveyed had a college education, and many of these held graduate degrees. Furthermore, of the remaining 9 percent, most had had some college training. It is reasonable to conclude that the typical arbitrator has had a significant amount of education.

The arbitrators ranged from 36 to 76 years old, and the average age was 53. It was impossible to obtain accurate information as to the length and breadth of experience of each arbitrator. However, many of the individuals contacted had spent most of their working lives in a particular industry or field, and were primarily asked to arbitrate cases in which this skill and experience was required. Although one cannot categorically state that most arbitrators are highly experienced men in their fields, it is possible to conclude that the typical arbitrator is a mature man who has been exposed to the business world for a number of years.

In summary, the 20,000 arbitrators in this country come from a variety of backgrounds. They can be characterized as mature, well-educated men with a number of years' experience in a given field.

WHY ARBITRATORS SERVE

One of the purposes of our survey of over 300 American Arbitration Association arbitrators was to determine what reasons influence a man to choose the arbitrator role. Arbitrators are normally volunteers who receive little or no compensation for their efforts. Without tangible incentives, the reasons for choosing to become an arbitrator are somewhat obscure.

In this section we will discuss the possible motivations of arbitrators which have been suggested by our investigations. It is our hope that this discussion will provide an insight into the kinds of men that constitute an arbitration tribunal.

In his book *Motivation and Personality,* A. H. Maslow discusses the factors which motivate people:

> Man is a wanting animal and rarely reaches a state of complete satisfaction except for a short time. As one desire is satisfied another pops up in its place. When this is satisfied, still another comes into the foreground, etc.

It is characteristic of the human being throughout his whole life that he is practically always desiring something.[2]

Maslow goes on to describe these desires as needs and then places them in a "hierarchy." He differentiates between the lower needs and higher needs. He defines the low needs as "far more localized, more tangible, and more limited than are higher needs"; lower needs include food, clothing, and shelter in contrast to higher needs of love and respect.

> The pursuit and the gratification of the higher needs have desirable *civic and social consequences*. To some extent, the higher the need the less selfish it must be. . . . People who have enough basic satisfaction to look for love and respect (rather than just food and safety) tend to develop such qualities as loyalty, friendliness, and *civic consciousness* and to become better parents, husbands, teachers, public servants, etc.[3] [Emphasis ours.]

As we have noted, arbitrators are mature persons and have acquired many years of business or professional experience. They have probably satisfied many of their material needs through success in their business or profession. In order to satisfy their higher needs, it is conceivable that they might seek opportunities outside their normal activities.

Our investigations indicate that the principal satisfaction achieved by the men who volunteer to be arbitrators is the feeling of fulfilling one's civic responsibility. One arbitrator responded, "I am content to serve without pay, in part because my schedule does not permit much other direct participation in 'civic' affairs (fund-raising, etc.). A citizen owes his community something without money reward."

Focusing more specifically on the type of civic responsibility the arbitrator thought he was fulfilling, our responses indicated that most arbitrators considered their role as a service to the *business community*. Their reasoning was that arbitration provides a low cost, timely, and convenient process for the settlement of business disputes and that this improves business relationships and the general "atmosphere" within which business transactions take place. Because of the requirement for special competence, the arbitrators often associate their service with the particular industry in which they do business. The arbitrator feels that he is making a contribution by performing his arbitrator role.

Another important reason for becoming an arbitrator was the desire to assist in relieving crowded court dockets. This attitude was primarily

[2] A. H. Maslow, *Motivation and Personality* (New York: Harper & Brothers, 1954), p. 69.
[3] *Ibid.*, p. 149.

expressed by lawyers, many of whom felt that arbitration could play a vital role in the future relief of the crowded dockets.

Those critical of commercial arbitration saw a less philanthropic purpose motivating the arbitrators. This argument was that the arbitrator role gave frustrated lawyers the chance to judge and wield a gavel. One of these critics stated: "Since the parties to arbitration are usually represented by counsel, lawyers who serve as arbitrators frequently react as if they were judges. In fact, I wouldn't be surprised if they thought they were judges." One arbitrator who had served on a panel with such a lawyer wrote, "Is there some way to screen out those attorneys who are frustrated judges, and will never attain that office?"

Since arbitration is only one of a variety of civic tasks in which one could fulfill a sense of civic responsibility, we must examine the differences which exist among these various affairs in order to work toward a hypothesis as to why arbitrators serve. Our respondents indicated some annoyance upon encountering the typical tasks of ticket selling, fund raising, or other duties which were far removed from the areas of their competence and experience. In contrast, the arbitrator, they say, is chosen for service on the basis of his skill and experience and has the opportunity to bring a valuable competence to his civic endeavor.

The arbitrator usually sets the time for the arbitration hearing; thus he can assure that it is held at his convenience. Arbitrators singled out this flexible timing aspect of arbitration as particularly desirable in order to avoid the pressure of civic responsibility during critical times in their own business. The only uncertainty or possible inconvenience connected with arbitration is that the length of the hearing cannot be established before the case is accepted. Although most cases are heard in one day, the length of the hearing is occasionally a problem, as indicated below.

The administrative body under whose auspices the arbitration is conducted accomplishes most of the detail work, thus obviating a common complaint about civic duties. For example, the American Arbitration Association handles all contact between the arbitrator and the parties involved, administers the proceeding, and provides assistance and support in carrying out the mechanical chores connected with arbitration.

Our research, however, does not suggest that the function of an arbitrator is without drawbacks. When queried in this regard, 40 percent of the arbitrators who responded to our questionnaire indicated they had been inconvenienced at one time or another. The items cited as causes for this trouble included hearings which ran for a number of days and the necessity for extensive periods of deliberation in order to arrive at an award.

In summary, our investigations indicate that frequently an arbitrator is attracted to arbitration because it affords him an opportunity to fulfill a civic responsibility. Arbitrators sometimes choose this role rather than other civic roles because it allows them to avoid some of the inconveniences and uncertainties commonly associated with other civic affairs. They feel their personal talents are used more effectively in arbitration. Some lawyers may be motivated by the confidence they have in their ability to judge. A number of people view arbitration as a public service contributing to the relief of crowded court dockets. It is conceivable that some arbitrators serve because they believe a certain amount of status attaches to the function and that, perhaps, it is good for their "image." Most arbitrators, however, seem to be satisfying a higher personal need by serving in this capacity.

ARBITRATOR COMPETENCE

The arbitrator is the key to the effectiveness of the commercial arbitration process. He must be able to judge on the basis of evidence and arrive at an equitable solution. The process is evaluated almost entirely on his performance. Since the role of the arbitrator is so critical, the competence of the arbitrator becomes a paramount issue in any consideration of commercial arbitration.

In order to estimate the degree of competence required of an arbitrator, we must first determine what is demanded of him in this role. It is then necessary to consider the personal characteristics which would enable him to perform effectively. Finally, we will examine the selection and development of arbitrators in this context and evaluate future approaches to improving the level of arbitrator competence in the future.

DEMANDS ON THE ARBITRATOR

One of the most significant demands imposed upon the arbitrator resides in the complexity of many commercial cases. This complexity involves both the nature of the dispute and the form of the proceeding.

Questions concerning the quality of a product, customer-supplier disagreements which are influenced by industry practices, and other such disputes require the arbitrator to have a complete grasp of industry practice, knowledge of products, and understanding of technology. The following comment by an attorney illustrates what is expected of an arbitrator: "One of the reasons that I recommended arbitration to my client is that his claim was difficult even to explain to the layman much less hope that he (the layman) comprehended its significance. I recognized the need to present the case to someone who would fully appreciate the situation."

Additionally, the arbitrator must resolve such procedural problems as conflicting or irrelevant testimony, lack of precedents, and the need to maintain order. He must also attempt to maintain the respect of the parties.

As an example of the demands placed on the arbitrator, the following is furnished from an arbitrator's actual experience:

> Situation: four partners, two on each side, with the question: "What was our agreement on the division of profit?" You might have believed either group, so plausible were the oral statements. Indeed, one side made a statement about the actions of another person who was not present at the hearing, and this statement was not challenged. Yet, it troubled me in typing my notes of what both parties had said, that the statement and actions did not make sense to me. I called another hearing and directed the absent person to appear and answer MY questions; the case fell into place instantly.
>
> From this early case, I learned:
>
> A. Take ample notes. Who said what?
>
> B. Do not let the case grow cold (and fuzzy). IMMEDIATELY sort it into groups of problems and sub-problems.
>
> C. Sort those notes into points agreed upon and points disagreed.
>
> This will indicate, at least, just exactly what is the key factor that the arbitrator really needs, for his conscience.

The arbitrator must assess each point of evidence, disregarding it or assimilating it, in building to his final decision. Since many of the arbitrators interviewed stated they admit all evidence, the magnitude of this problem can be great. Many feel, however, that this is a desirable feature of commercial arbitration. In fact, one arbitrator said, "I firmly believe that it [arbitration] is a better method than jury trial in most cases. The rules of arbitration are not bound by legal evidence." Therefore, the arbitrator *has* to establish his own priorities on the relevancy of the information presented.

The proceeding is also subject to problems of a legal nature. Our research indicates that, in about 25 percent of the cases heard, an arbitrator is confronted with legal matters as significant parts of the dispute. These legal points (for example, legal interpretation of contract wording) require skillful handling and often require a familiarity with contract law. In addition, the arbitrator must conduct the proceeding in an orderly fashion and create an atmosphere conducive to gentlemanly conduct. This requires tactful assertion of authority. It can be seen that the demands placed upon the arbitrator are many, varied, and complex.

ARBITRATOR CHARACTERISTICS

In view of the considerable demands placed upon the arbitrator, it is necessary to define the characteristics needed to cope with such demands. Professor James J. Healy, renowned arbitrator, describes the successful practitioner as one who should—

- a. by temperament not be emotional. He should maintain a certain sense of aloofness by remaining above the arguments and pleas of an emotional nature, and thereby separating the emotional issues from fact.

- b. possess a capacity to think logically. He should be able to investigate the facts presented in a case and to reach a reasonable conclusion based upon correct or reliable inference.

- c. be objective. He should attempt to be free of personal feelings or prejudice.

- d. be open-minded. He should be receptive to new arguments and ideas.

- e. be capable of establishing priorities on the relevancy of information.

- f. possess firmness. He should not be so firm as to dominate the proceeding; however, he should exercise control over the direction and activities during the proceeding.

- g. exhibit patience. He should be calm and persevere quietly when testimony is being given.

- h. be familiar with legal proceedings. He should have had at least one course in Contract Law or experience in this field. He should at least be familiar with rules of evidence.

- i. have a mature appearance.

- j. not be financially dependent on arbitration for a living.

The above are general characteristics relating to all arbitrators. Our investigations would lead us to add to the list: Possess expertise and experience in the field to which the dispute relates. In fact, if these factors were rated in priority, most arbitrators would place expertise near the top. Our research also indicated a feeling by some proponents of arbitration that arbitrator expertise is a major advantage of arbitration. Some went so far as to say that expertise combined with dedication and a desire to be fair are the only characteristics needed by a qualified arbitrator. It was expressed this way:

Arbitrators are not judges in a court but in fact are more qualified than judges. They can be fair because they are not political appointees, and they have a sense of responsibility to themselves and their industry. They are knowledgeable of their industry and its practices. What other traits does a good arbitrator need?

While business experience and honorable motives are vital ingredients to the arbitration process, we would not suggest that they are the only characteristics needed to cope with the demands of arbitration.

An article in *The Arbitration Journal* dealt with this subject. The commentator described a view expressed by the Honorable Charles D. Breitel:[4]

Judge Breitel pointed out that not every man of intelligence, goodwill and disinterestedness is necessarily a good arbitrator. Personality traits also play an important part. Arbitration is an adversary proceeding, the outcome of which often has serious economic consequences for the parties. The atmosphere may become highly charged, so an arbitrator must be able to listen to the parties, keep firm control of proceedings, and form an opinion uninfluenced by emotion.

The possession of these characteristics by the arbitrator is critical to the effectiveness of the process. However, it is highly unlikely that all businessmen possess these characteristics to the same degree. As a result, it is reasonable to expect that the process used to select arbitrators would consider the need for men with certain skills and characteristics. One would expect to find a program for developing these characteristics in those men already arbitrating. It is to this matter of selection and development that we now turn.

ARBITRATOR SELECTION

Arbitrators go through two selection processes—appointment to a panel and selection as an arbitrator. The first process is initiated by an invitation from an organization, such as the American Arbitration Association, to serve on its panel of arbitrators. The second selection is made by the party to a dispute in choosing an arbitrator to hear a particular case. Both of these selection processes will be examined and evaluated below.

The panel selection procedure presently employed by the American Arbitration Association is informal and flexible. Arbitrators are most frequently added to the rolls as a result of the recommendation of another arbitrator. The prospective arbitrator is asked to fill out an application on

[4] An editorial, "A Tribute to Commercial Arbitrators," *The Arbitration Journal,* Vol. 15, No. 1 (1960), p. 1.

which he lists such information as date of birth, profession, and education. The Association depends solely upon the sponsor's judgment as to the qualification of the applicant. These applications are automatically approved, and the new arbitrator's name is added to the arbitrator panel.

In contrast to the panel selection method, the procedure for choosing an arbitrator on a specific case is more formal and inflexible.

As an example, excerpts from the American Arbitration Association procedure are cited:

QUALIFICATIONS OF ARBITRATOR
No person shall serve as an Arbitrator in any arbitration if he has any financial or personal interest in the result of the arbitration, unless the parties, in writing, waive such disqualification.

APPOINTMENT FROM PANEL
If the parties have not appointed an Arbitrator and have not provided any other method of appointment, the Arbitrator shall be appointed in the following manner: Immediately after the filing of the Demand or Submission, the American Arbitration Association shall submit simultaneously to each party to the dispute an identical list of names of persons chosen from the Panel. Each party to the dispute shall have seven days from the mailing date in which to cross off any names to which he objects, number the remaining names indicating the order of his preference, and return the list to the American Arbitration Association. If a party does not return the list within the time specified, all persons named therein shall be deemed acceptable. From among the persons who have been approved on both lists, and in accordance with the designated order of mutual preference, the American Arbitration Association shall invite the acceptance of an Arbitrator to serve. If the parties fail to agree upon any of the persons named, or if acceptable Arbitrators are unable to act, or if for any other reason the appointment cannot be made from the submitted lists, the American Arbitration Association shall have the power to make the appointment from other members of the Panel without the submission of any additional lists.

DIRECT APPOINTMENT BY PARTIES
If the agreement of the parties names an Arbitrator or specifies a method of appointing an Arbitrator, that designation or method shall be followed. The notice of appointment, with name and address of such Arbitrator, shall be filed with the American Arbitration Association by the appointing party. Upon request of any such appointing party, the American Arbitration Association shall submit a list of members from the Panel from which the party may, if he so desires, make the appointment.

If the agreement specifies a period of time within which an Arbitrator shall be appointed, and any party fails to make such appointment within that period, the American Arbitration Association shall make the appointment. If no period of time is specified in the agreement, the American

Arbitration Association shall notify the parties to make the appointment and if within seven days thereafter such Arbitrator has not been so appointed, the American Arbitration Association shall make the appointment.

NUMBER OF ARBITRATORS
If the arbitration agreement does not specify the number of Arbitrators, the disputes shall be heard and determined by one Arbitrator, unless the American Arbitration Association, in its discretion, directs that a greater number of Arbitrators be appointed.

NOTICE TO ARBITRATOR OF HIS APPOINTMENT
Notice of the appointment of the neutral Arbitrator, whether appointed by the parties or by the American Arbitration Association, shall be mailed to the Arbitrator by the American Arbitration Association, together with a copy of these Rules, and the signed acceptance of the Arbitrator shall be filed prior to the opening of the first hearing.

DISCLOSURE BY ARBITRATOR OF DISQUALIFICATION
Prior to accepting his appointment, the prospective neutral Arbitrator shall disclose any circumstances likely to create a presumption of bias or which he believes might disqualify him as an impartial Arbitrator. Upon receipt of such information, the American Arbitration Association shall immediately disclose it to the parties who, if willing to proceed under the circumstances disclosed, shall so advise the American Arbitration Association in writing. If either party declines to waive the presumptive disqualification, the vacancy thus created shall be filled in accordance with the applicable provisions of these Rules.

TIME AND PLACE
The Arbitrator shall fix the time and place for each hearing. The American Arbitration Association shall mail to each party notice thereof at least five days in advance, unless the parties by mutual agreement waive such notice or modify the terms thereof.

The procedures used by various administrative organizations (for example, the American Arbitration Association, trade associations, and stock exchanges) are not necessarily alike. Many procedural differences are involved and include such major elements as the degree of freedom allowed the parties in making the selection. While the American Arbitration Association allows the parties to select the arbitrator privately, many trade associations appoint the arbitrator and the parties do not participate in the selection.

It appears that there are only two places where the qualifications of an arbitrator candidate can be evaluated. First, the person who recommends the prospective arbitrator obviously makes a judgment concerning the man's qualifications. The problem here is that there is hardly any way of establishing objective criteria for making such a judgment. It is difficult to evaluate such characteristics as objectivity, open-mindedness, and sanguinity. The only skills that seem susceptible to evaluation are knowledge of the law and expertise in a particular field.

Second, the parties to an arbitration can make a judgment as to an arbitrator's qualifications at the time of his selection for the case. However, this judgment is complicated by the fact that most commercial arbitrators do not have reputations as expert arbitrators, and many are not well known in the industry. Thus many times parties must choose arbitrators from a list which does not contain a name that they recognize. (Attorneys for parties may investigate the reputation of men listed, but this normally occurs only when the case is of major consequence.) In one of our interviews a businessman stated: "You can talk all you want about judging an arbitrator's skill before he is selected; in my case neither my lawyer nor myself had ever heard of anyone on the list sent by the Association. What kind of judgments about skill can I make under those circumstances?"

In spite of this difficulty, our research indicates that arbitrators are chosen because of their presumed knowledge in a particular field. Of the arbitrators surveyed, 90 percent of businessmen arbitrators and 60 percent of the lawyer arbitrators felt the choice was made because of expertise in the field. In addition, 75 percent of the arbitration participants responded that they chose an arbitrator with a specific competence because they felt he would bring the required skills to the tribunal.

ARBITRATOR DEVELOPMENT

Under the present systems, there are few formal arbitrator training or apprenticeship programs. Moreover, arbitrators are expected to develop their skills either by arbitrating or through their own business and educational experiences. In any case the responsibility for development and training rests with the arbitrator himself. Thus the selection process, as described above, does not guarantee qualified men, and there is no formal machinery to train them after they have been selected.

Even though many of the desired arbitrator characteristics are innate, they can be sharpened through training or experience. Conceivably, the person who possesses some of these characteristics can become more competent in applying them to different situations through practice and experience. Such experience can be obtained either through an educational process or actual exposure to arbitration. Our investigations, however, indicated that arbitrators hear an average of approximately one case per year, and most cases last one day. Thus present exposure as an arbitrator is not frequent enough to develop the necessary characteristics to any significant degree.

FUTURE ARBITRATOR SELECTION, DEVELOPMENT, AND COMPENSATION

It would be relatively impossible to evaluate the degree to which an individual possessed the characteristics necessary to make him a good arbitrator. Perhaps through psychological testing and interviewing, the data with which to make this judgment could be obtained. However, such measurement would be expensive, time consuming, and often inconclusive. Furthermore, the potential arbitrators would probably resent such a process.

Formal training of arbitrators, while not impossible, would be very difficult. Such training would probably require repetitive exposure to arbitral proceedings and would involve a good deal of the trainee's time. It is unlikely that a person performing a public service would be able, much less willing, to sacrifice so much of his time without adequate compensation.

Compensation of commercial arbitrators is a subject which has been debated for years. Proponents argue that adequate compensation would foster the development of a cadre of professional commercial arbitrators who would be widely reputed, experienced, and well qualified. Opponents argue that the necessity for compensation would eliminate one of the principal advantages of commercial arbitration—economy.

There are further questions. Would a financial incentive attract a more capable arbitrator than would a social incentive? Is it practical to institutionalize the commercial arbitrator's role? While in labor arbitration there is a cadre of professional, paid arbitrators, there are basic differences which inhibit us from generalizing from the labor experience. First, businessmen arbitrators who are expert in their fields are often allowed by their companies to serve because such service contributes to the public or industry good. This public-service motivation might be eliminated if commercial arbitrators were paid, and there might actually occur a reduction in the number of arbitrators available. Secondly, commercial cases in particular fields could arise so infrequently that it would not be feasible to attempt to maintain professional commercial arbitrators in each of these areas.

There are no easy answers to the questions of arbitrator selection, development, and compensation. A later chapter, however, will suggest means by which businessmen can help work toward effective solutions.

We have noted that the arbitrator is the key to the effectiveness of the commercial arbitration process. Therefore, the competence of the arbitrator is a vital consideration. In accomplishing his role, the commercial arbitrator must deal with two levels of complexity—the complexity of the issues in the dispute and the complexity related to procedural matters. The arbitrator faces a formidable task in attempting to operate within this complex environment. In order to perform this task effectively, the arbitrator should possess certain characteristics, as well as exhibit an ability in a specific field.

The selection and development of arbitrators with these skills is critical to the effectiveness of the arbitration process. The existing procedures for selection and development do not adequately insure a high level of arbitrator competence. Although we do not suggest a solution to this dilemma, there is a need for a system which would minimize the risk of employing unqualified arbitrators. There also seems to be a need for a more formalized development program for arbitrators and consideration of such a program raises this question: Should commercial arbitrators be compensated?

THE ARBITRATOR'S ATTITUDES

The arbitrator's attitudes, to be discussed here, provide an interesting contrast with the businessman's views in Chapter II and the lawyer's views to be covered in Chapter IV. In the presentation of our research findings on the arbitrator's attitudes, we will focus primarily on two areas—his views of the arbitrator's role and his views toward the arbitration process.

ARBITRATOR VIEWS HIS ROLE

In an effort to obtain an overall idea of how the arbitrators thought they were performing, we asked them "Do you feel in most cases the parties are satisfied with the conduct of the hearing?" Ninety-seven percent responded positively. The few negative responses were given by an equal percentage of businessmen and lawyers. The major reasons given for answering yes were: comments by the parties, general attitudes of the parties, and absence of protests.

Time demands. As was pointed out in the section on arbitrator competence, there are time constraints and uncertainties which cause the individual arbitrator some inconvenience. In response to the question "Have you found any difficulty with accepting a case you thought was going to require up to one day [only to find] it required longer?" 40 percent of the arbitrators indicated they had. However, because the arbitrator can select the time of the hearing at his own convenience, this problem is not as great as it might at first seem. Of these same men, 97 percent indicated that the time factor had no influence on the amount of effort put into a case.

Over 95 percent of arbitrators contacted indicated satisfaction with the manner in which administrative functions are handled by the arbitration agency—for example, by the American Arbitration Association. Furthermore, the small number of recommended changes also indicates that the arbitrator is pleased with the administrative services rendered to him. The arbitrator viewed the American Arbitration Association as effectively protecting him from petty inconveniences.

Mediation. One might think that mediation would offer a means by which an arbitrator could save the parties and himself some time. Successful mediation efforts might provide a settlement which would be satisfactory to both parties. On the contrary, however, 62 percent of the arbitrators responded that mediation was not a part of their role and they were opposed to it. A typical view was expressed this way: "I would disqualify such an arbitrator, who attempted to mediate. By the time of arbitration, all compromise possibilities have long since been exhausted and each side is determined to win."

In spite of this majority opinion concerning mediation, more than 20 percent of the arbitrators had attempted mediation at one time or another. The reason for this was that in certain circumstances the possibility of successful mediation outweighed the risk of failure. The type of circumstances referred to were described this way by one arbitrator: "The parties had almost made an agreement while I was sitting there like a fool trying to arbitrate."

The problem with mediation, however, is that the arbitrator becomes a friend to both parties and is made privy to information that might not otherwise be presented to him. If his mediation efforts were to fail, it would be extremely difficult for him to change hats again and deal with only that information and evidence which would be offered at the subsequent arbitration hearing. When the arbitrator gambles on mediation, he may be destroying his usefulness as an arbitrator.

Compromise. A discussion of the various meanings we ascribe to the word "compromise" was included in Chapter II. The two types of compromise to which we referred were honorific and invidious compromise. Invidious compromise is considered to be "splitting the difference" without much reference to the facts of the case. Honorific compromise is an objective and reasoned decision which happened to fall between the two claimants' positions.

In order to determine how arbitrators felt about compromise as a part of arbitration, we asked, in our questionnaires and interviews, whether their decisions were compromises. Forty-three percent answered affirmatively and 50 percent indicated their decisions were clearly in favor of one party. The remaining 7 percent did not commit themselves, and we would speculate this was because of a difficulty in defining the compromise concept. From this data we conclude that many arbitrators see compromise as an inescapable part of the function they perform.

However, one of the more outspoken arbitrator critics of compromise stated his objection this way: "Although I agree with the principles of arbitration, I am disgusted by the way some of my colleagues implement these principles. Not only can the arbitrators be poor judges, but they too frequently cloud their decision by attempting to satisfy everyone through compromise, and end up actually hurting all parties in the process." This man rejects invidious compromise as having no place in arbitration.

Another response suggested that compromise was an outgrowth of arbitrator incompetence in many situations:

> The arbitrator often hears irrelevant testimony. If he is not adept at segregating this testimony and establishing priorities on its relevancy, he will likely become confused. When he makes his decision on the case, the issue will be unclear unless this confusion is eliminated. If this occurs, the arbitrator will consciously split the difference and compromise the award. Moreover, since his decision is final, he can compromise without fear of consequence.

However, in no case did any of the arbitrators who viewed their decisions as compromises suggest that invidious compromise (splitting the difference) was their purpose.

ATTORNEY AS ARBITRATOR

Why do certain critics of commercial arbitration suggest that lawyers serve as arbitrators for the ego satisfying feeling of being "judge for a day"? Their argument goes something like this. The lawyer sees commercial arbitration in terms of his own world, the world of litigation and the courtroom. The lawyer must naturally view the role of the arbitrator who sits in judgment over two adversaries as being similar to the role of the jurist. In fact, a proponent of arbitration, Judge Nathan Clayton, recommends that lawyers "learn how the judicial mind works" by arbitrating:

> I would also urge you—particularly the younger lawyers—to make your-
> selves available as arbitrators. You will find it a rewarding experience, and
> you will "learn by doing" how the judicial mind works. If it is true that
> most lawyers dream of becoming judges, there is no better way for you
> to learn whether you would really like judicial work. And there is probably
> no better way for the Bar to learn whether a lawyer is good judicial timber.
> The day may not be very far off when the appointing powers will consider
> recruiting some of our judges from the ranks of experienced arbitrators.[5]

Since the position of judge is a worthy professional aspiration for an
attorney, it is logical to assume that the lawyer would enjoy playing out
his ambitions in the arbitral tribunal. It is hard to say whether this
argument has any veracity. There does seem to be some indication that the
lawyer sees himself as operating in a *professional* capacity as arbitrator
while he sees the businessman as operating as an amateur. Perhaps it is
difficult for a lawyer to envision the layman as a judge. One lawyer said,
"Arbitrating is a natural extension of my livelihood. I have to deal with
similar problems on a day-to-day basis. I am sure there are some unqualified people arbitrating. . . . I doubt if these people have to deal with
similar situations in their businesses." It seems strange that a lawyer would
be blind to the fact that when a businessman arbitrates a technical dispute
he is employing the skills of his profession to the same extent as when the
lawyer judges an objection to a point of evidence. This blind spot toward
the layman might lend some slight support to the theory that when the
lawyer looks at the arbitrator's chair he sees the judge's bench.

Arbitrators are volunteers and are not paid for their services. The
question of whether they should be paid is debated by both proponents
and opponents of commercial arbitration and has been discussed earlier.
The arbitrator's views on this subject were interesting. The responses by
130 American Arbitration Association arbitrators (48 lawyers and 82
businessmen) to the compensation question are summarized as follows:

"Should lawyer arbitrators be compensated?"

Response by:	Yes	No
Lawyers	74%	26%
Nonlawyers	46	54
Combined response	57	43

---

[5] Judge Nathan Clayton, "Arbitration: Substantial Justice in Private Disputes,"
The Arbitration Journal, Vol. 12, No. 4 (1957), p. 203. An address before the
Bar Association of the District of Columbia.

"Should businessmen arbitrators be compensated?"

Response by:	Yes	No
Lawyers	65%	35%
Nonlawyers	23	77
Combined response	39	61

The conclusions from these responses are: the majority of lawyer arbitrators feel that all arbitrators should be paid. The nonlawyers are almost evenly divided in their views toward paying lawyer arbitrators but for the most part believe that nonlawyer arbitrators should not be paid. We can speculate that businessmen and lawyers associate the lawyer's time with money and the businessman's with fulfilling a civic obligation.

Thirty-five percent of those who favored compensating lawyers gave as their reason "the lawyer's time is money." In several interviews, this point was also underscored. When queried as to why they did not associate a businessman's time away from his business with money, many responded that the businessman is performing a service to his particular industry and the time-loss argument is not pertinent. On one occasion a lawyer stated, "The businessman's business continues to operate while he is arbitrating; but the lawyer's business as an adviser and counselor ceases when he is away."

ARBITRATOR VIEWS THE PROCESS

Strengths and weaknesses. In an attempt to obtain an assessment of the arbitration process from the arbitrator's standpoint, we asked each arbitrator to indicate what he thought were the advantages and disadvantages of commercial arbitration.

It is significant to note that no single advantage emerged as being of overwhelming importance. The advantages, however, fell into three distinct groupings, as indicated below:

Advantages	Total Response(%)
Expertise of arbitrators	30
Time saving	29
Cost saving	12
Fairness	8
Informality	7
Relief from courts	7
Legal assistance not needed	4
Maintenance of relationships	2
Convenience to parties	1

The arbitrators considered their unique skills as one of the most important characteristics of the process. This assessment of the value of the arbitrator's service is supported by the data from businessman questionnaires cited in Chapter II. Time savings and expertise were listed as advantages by 59 percent of the respondents. The second grouping did not receive one-half as much emphasis as the first. Arbitrators felt that the attributes of commercial arbitration were best utilized in disputes over quality, damage, and breach of contract.

The following table presents the arbitrator's views on the weaknesses of the process:

Disadvantages	*Percent of Total Response*
Lack of public knowledge and acceptance	36
Lack of preparation by the parties	22
Lack of experience and understanding of commercial arbitration by lawyers representing parties	20
Compromise by arbitrators too often	8
Lack of legal training by arbitrators	7
Poor selection of arbitrators	7

The arbitrators thought that the lack of public knowledge and acceptance was by far the greatest weakness of the process. Criticism of the adequacy of preparation by the parties and of the extent of the lawyers' experience and understanding indicates that the arbitrators are concerned with the performance of the other participants in the arbitration process.

A weakness of commercial arbitration commented upon by many attorneys is the absence of written opinions. These attorneys claim that the necessity for written opinions would make arbitrators devote more thoughtful consideration to the analysis of the cases, and the parties would know why they had won or lost. We asked the arbitrators for their attitudes toward written opinions. Seventy-five percent of the arbitrators indicated that they favored rules not requiring written opinions. The most common reasons were the burdensome nature of the opinions and the fact that arbitrators generally, with the exception of attorneys, are not practiced writers of adjudicated opinions. Most arbitrators do not feel written opinions would add to the process, and many feel that a requirement for such an opinion would also require compensation.

Arbitrators feel that the attributes of commercial arbitration were least utilized in disputes where points of law were relevant. In an interview with an arbitrator the following comment was made: "I do not personally feel that I would be qualified to decide such a dispute [over point of law]; however, a person with legal training would be qualified. Fortunately, the only time I have heard that kind of disagreement was when I was on a panel with a lawyer." Another arbitrator pointed out that "I have a strong conviction that arbitration is not a panacea and it *must* be used discriminately." However, there was one vocal dissenter who said: "There really aren't any disputes that I can think of to which commercial arbitration is not applicable. . . . Sure I think commercial arbitration is appropriate for settling disputes on conflicting testimony. Why not? Judges are no more qualified than we are." Such an attitude was in the minority.

Arbitration boards. As was indicated in the section on arbitrator selection, the tribunal boards vary in size, depending on the rules being used. Most commonly, these boards are of one, three, and five men. The board may be composed entirely of neutrals or may have representatives of the parties on it.

Of the arbitrators we surveyed and interviewed, 26 had served as neutrals on boards of arbitration containing representatives of the parties. None of them thought this type of board was advantageous, and 18 stated that one arbitrator could have handled the hearing just as easily and effectively. Eight of them specifically mentioned, "The representatives only confused the issue."

Inquiries concerning multiman boards where all arbitrators are neutrals drew a somewhat different response. Of the 130 arbitrators who replied, 95 had served on this type of board; to the question "Do you have a preference between serving as the only arbitrator or a member of a board of arbitration?" the following response was given by the latter group:

Preference	Number of Responses	Percent
Only arbitrator	17	18
Board of arbitration	43	50
No preference	35	32

To the question "Do you feel that a board of arbitration (all neutrals) should be used in more or fewer cases?" the response was as follows:

Preference	Number of Responses	Percent
More	52	55
Fewer	43	45

These responses indicate modified support for the three-man neutral board. Some of the comments received demonstrate the arbitrators' feelings toward the advantages of a three-man neutral board.

In support of boards, one arbitrator stated:

> I have served as a neutral on a board of arbitration several times and also as a single arbitrator. From the arbitrator's point of view, I prefer the board, and in fact, favor more extensive use of it. The parties are given a fairer hearing since there are two representatives from the trade who can handle the trade issues and there is usually a lawyer who can handle the legal questions. I have also had occasion to be party to a dispute. In my case, I specifically requested that a three-man board hear the case.

A contrary view was offered by another arbitrator on a three-man board that included an attorney:

> The attorney naturally became our chairman and did all the talking and ran the case—and the Association knows that I will never again serve as a silent nonentity. Make no mistake; I have the highest regard for the overwhelming majority of attorneys whom I know with great intimacy in 30 years of CPA experience. I would serve on a panel if any of my dozens of attorney-friends were co-panelists; or if I could extract a promise regarding the conduct of the proceedings. But, in conclusion, it is my observation that nine-man Supreme Courts are for constitutional issues, and trial courts are all run by one man.

Other opinions were received which indicated that most men felt that each type of board had its own advantages. The three-man neutral board was said to be superior because all panelists had a common goal. Disadvantages of the three-man (versus one-man) neutral panel were encountered in coordinating the time of the hearing and in the possibility of one arbitrator dominating the proceeding.

* * *

The arbitrator is the key to the effectiveness of the arbitration process. Arbitrators come from a variety of backgrounds and bring the quality of expertise to the tribunal. A typical arbitrator is mature and well educated; most serve to fulfill a need to discharge a civic responsibility. They choose to do this by serving as arbitrators because the role is convenient and makes use of their particular talents. The role of the arbitrator is not easy. It makes heavy demands on time, it requires skill, and, in order to be performed effectively, it requires such intangible attributes as objectivity, open-mindedness, an ability to rank relevant information in priority order, some familiarity with legal procedure, and, of course, technical expertise.

The existing selection process does not necessarily guarantee the presence of these characteristics, and the development of a professional class of commercial arbitrators is inhibited by such realities as the necessity for compensation.

The arbitrator is satisfied with his own performance, is partially in favor of compensation, recognizes that compromise is part of arbitration, but believes that mediation is not. He considers that the strengths of the process lie in his own expertise and in the speed of resolution provided. He sees a lack of public knowledge and acceptance as the major weakness of commercial arbitration.

The implications for the potential of commercial arbitration are twofold:

1. The arbitration process depends upon the competence of the arbitrator, and currently this cannot be guaranteed by the selection and development processes.

2. Public knowledge and acceptance of commercial arbitration must be strengthened in order to insure its future. However, public knowledge and acceptance depends to a very great extent on the attitudes of lawyers who are exercising a growing influence over the process. These attitudes and this influence are the subject of Chapter IV.

CHAPTER IV

THE LAWYER AND
COMMERCIAL ARBITRATION •

T HE ROLE OF THE MODERN CORPORATION LAWYER began to evolve in the 1890's when the rapidly expanding number of corporate formations required the lawyer's skills in drafting documents and conducting negotiations. Since that time, the relationship between the American legal and business communities has become increasingly close. The tremendous importance of the lawyer today in the business world is attested to by the number of corporations that maintain their own legal departments staffed with salaried lawyers and by the number of large law firms in metropolitan areas that cater to the business world.

THE LAWYER AND BUSINESS ORGANIZATIONS

This development was the focus of an address given in 1934 by Harlan F. Stone, late Chief Justice of the United States, who stated the belief that the best skill and capacity of the legal community had been drawn into the service of business and finance. In commenting upon the growing dependence of business upon the lawyer, Stone made the following assertion: "The intricacies of business organization are built upon a legal framework which the current growth of administrative law is still further elaborating. Without the constant advice and guidance of lawyers business would come to an abrupt halt."[1]

In this elevated position of importance, today's corporate lawyer focuses upon mixed questions of both law and business. His role carries him into the areas of policy-making and planning for the future, as well as into the more traditional areas of legal concern: "In big business the practice is much more prevalent of consulting the lawyer before rather than after the act, particularly in well-managed corporations which make enlightened

[1] Harlan F. Stone, "The Public Influence of the Bar" (1934), 48 *Harvard Law Review,* p. 9.

use of their lawyers. In such corporations the manager demands the protection of a lawyer's blessing before he embarks on a new program."[2]

The influence of the legal community upon the business world is heightened by the widespread practice of seeking lawyers to serve as corporation directors or as members of top management in large corporations. Thus it becomes important to examine closely the attitudes of the legal profession toward commercial arbitration. Not only is the lawyer often placed in the position of settling disputes through arbitration, but his voice has become increasingly influential in the basic decision of whether to utilize the process. Clearly, the degree of acceptance currently enjoyed by commercial arbitration on the part of the legal profession will be of significant impact in determining its future.

It would be incorrect to infer from the foregoing that the developing relationship between the legal and business communities has resulted in a one-way pattern of influence. Rather, the realities of business conditions and the need for successful managers to respond to those conditions have become increasingly felt by lawyers serving business. The necessity for this sensitivity became apparent early in the evolution of the corporation lawyer. In referring to the changes in American commerce at the turn of the century and the resultant pressure brought to bear on the lawyer, Robert Swaine states:

> There was a new tempo. In the earlier days high pressure had been infrequent. A trial or argument could go over to suit the convenience of counsel. But bankers who took large financial commitments in the purchase of securities were subject to the vagaries of the market; their counsel were under constant pressure to conclude the necessary proceedings with the greatest possible dispatch.[3]

Thus the lawyer, as influential a personality in business as he has become, has not reached his present position without adapting to constraints outside of his trade. This has been particularly true in the handling of commercial disputes. Swaine comments upon this development:

> Big Business of today is less litigious than were the rugged individual merchants and manufacturers of the old days. The modern corporate client expects its business to be handled as to keep it out of the courts. As a result most lawyers today devote the large part of their efforts in avoiding litigation rather than conducting it. . . . The function of those

---

[2] Glen McDaniel, "Ethical Problems of Counsel for Big Business, The Burden of Resolving Conflicting Interests" (1952), 38 *American Bar Association Journal*, p. 257.
[3] See Robert T. Swaine, "Impact of Big Business on the Profession: An Answer to Critics of the Modern Bar" (1949), 35 *American Bar Association Journal*, p. 89.

of us who serve industry, trade, and finance is not alone to keep them technically within the law, but to do our part toward keeping them functioning smoothly. . . .[4]

In looking to the future, one has little reason to suspect that the corporate lawyer will need to be any less sensitive and able to adapt to the constraints of the commercial world in order to meet the needs of his client. Nor is there any evidence to predict that he will be unwilling to do so. As will be explored later in this chapter, such a trend could be important to the future of commercial arbitration.

THE LAWYER AND BUSINESS DISPUTES

The settlement of disputes which have escalated beyond the stage of informal settlement by the two parties has traditionally been entrusted to the capabilities of the lawyer. In addition, as pointed out above, the business manager has come to rely heavily upon the lawyer's advice on how future disputes can be avoided, or if they do arise, how they should be settled. The extent of this dependence was tested in the spring of 1965 by a questionnaire circulated to participants in the Advanced Management Program at the Harvard Business School. As was stated in Chapter II, one of the questions asked was "Who in the company should make decisions concerning business disputes?" Of those responding, no less than 85 percent answered, "The general manager and legal counsel, with the general manager controlling." The balance (about 15 percent) answered, "The general manager and legal counsel, with counsel controlling." It is interesting to note that none of the respondents (all experienced business managers) felt that the legal counsel should be excluded from such decisions.

In turning more specifically to the decision of whether to employ commercial arbitration, it was similarly found that lawyers play an important role. In a second questionnaire, circulated to business managers throughout the country who had used commercial arbitration, the following question was posed: "What has been the source of your advice to use or not to use commercial arbitration?" Of 89 who answered the question, 29 cited their legal staff as the source, and 25 cited outside counsel. Of the remaining respondents, 12 relied upon trade associations for their advice, and 23 made the decision on either personal preference, or personal preference confirmed by legal advice.

These findings confirmed what we were tempted to take for granted—

---

[4] *Ibid.,* p. 169.

that the lawyer is a major governing figure in commercial disputes. What we did find to be enlightening was the extent of the seasoned business manager's reliance upon legal counsel in determining how disputes are to be settled. Above all, it underlines the importance of the attitudes of the legal community upon the current and future use of commercial arbitration.

THE LAWYER IN TRIBUNALS

We have looked at the importance of the lawyer's role in business and at the strength of his influence in determining how commercial disputes should be resolved. This question now arises: What is his role in the actual process settlement, if the choice to use commercial arbitration is made?

There are two roles which lawyers do assume in commercial arbitration tribunals. The first is that of being an arbitrator. In tribunals held under the auspices of the American Arbitration Association, 20 percent of the cases are heard by arbitrators who have a legal background. The issues that this practice raises will be dealt with later in this chapter and have, to some extent, been discussed already in Chapter III. The second role that the lawyer can assume in the arbitration tribunal is that of representing his client. It is this second role with which we are concerned here.

The use of legal counsel to represent the adversaries in commercial arbitration varies widely with the institutional setting in which the proceeding is held. In her study of commercial arbitration, Soia Mentschikoff found that of the self-contained trade associations with internal mechanisms for arbitration, 40 percent explicitly discouraged or forbade the use of an attorney representative. She also found that in the remaining 60 percent, legal representation was a rarity.[5] Furthermore, in a questionnaire sent by the authors to 1,673 trade associations in the spring of 1965, this question was posed: "Is representation by counsel: forbidden by rules; permitted if party provides notice of intention to Association; no limitation upon privilege; or encouraged?" Of the associations that responded to the question, all stated that legal representation was not encouraged in their arbitration proceedings.

The opposite is found true in the case of the American Arbitration Association's machinery, in which attorneys are used the majority of the time. Mentschikoff found lawyers representing their clients in about 80 percent of the cases resolved under the American Arbitration Association.[6]

[5] Soia Mentschikoff, "Commercial Arbitration" (1961), 61 *Columbia Law Review,* p. 857.
[6] *Ibid.,* p. 859.

This figure was confirmed by a questionnaire sent by the authors to businessmen who had been involved in cases held under the American Arbitration Association. To the question "Is legal counsel used in commercial arbitration proceedings?" 61 of 79 respondents (77 percent) replied "yes."

The reasons for this striking contrast of opinions as to the desirability of legal representation in commercial arbitration were numerous and varied.

The American Arbitration Association openly encourages lawyer participation at all steps of the arbitration procedure, from the drafting of arbitration clauses in contracts through the hearing itself. In a pamphlet published by the Association, this encouragement is readily apparent. In speaking of contractual clauses, the Association states: "The skills of the lawyer are in demand at every step of the arbitration process, but nowhere more urgently than in the drafting of the arbitration clause."[7] The Association goes on to state: "But between the right to arbitrate and the winning of an arbitral award there is often a gap which only the skill, experience, and judgment of a lawyer can bridge."[8]

To buttress its position on the importance and desirability of legal representatives, the American Arbitration Association quotes Whitney North Seymour, former president of the American Bar Association, as follows:

> I have always believed that an ability to conduct arbitration effectively is a very important part of a lawyer's equipment. The arbitration hearing room is, increasingly, one of the many forums of adjudication that the lawyer must practice in if he is to serve his clients, and this field of activity calls for all his professional skills.[9]

To a great extent, it appears that the American Arbitration Association bases its beliefs on the degree of similarity it sees between duties performed in taking a case to arbitration and to litigation. In drawing this comparison, the American Arbitration Association cites the selection of arbitrators as being akin to the empaneling of jurors in that both "call for the same insight and understanding of issues and men."[10] As in litigation, documents and exhibits must be prepared, there are papers to be subpoenaed, and briefs on facts to be written. The American Arbitration Association feels that skill in marshaling facts, examining and cross-examining witnesses, and arguing cases in a logical and persuasive manner are as essential facets in winning a case in arbitration as in litigation.

---

[7] American Arbitration Association, *The Lawyer and Arbitration* (pamphlet), July 1964, p. 6.
[8] *Ibid.*, p. 7.
[9] *Ibid.*, inside cover.
[10] *Ibid.*, p. 7.

The American Arbitration Association points out further the parallels between the progression of a case in its arbitration tribunals and court procedure. Customarily, both sides will make opening statements, examine and cross-examine witnesses, introduce exhibits, and make final summations. On these bases, the American Arbitration Association feels that "These are tasks for which the lawyer's training especially qualifies him, in private tribunals no less than in courts of law."[11] This reasoning leads the Association to believe that the lawyer who is familiar with commercial arbitration's characteristics and useful applications is in the best position to use it effectively: "Arbitration produces the best results in the hands of the lawyer who understands its uses, its limits, and its own rules of procedure."[12]

Aside from those reasons given by the American Arbitration Association to support legal representation, there are those which relate to the attorney's ability to argue a case effectively under conditions of pressure and emotion. One lawyer we interviewed summed it up in this way:

> It's questionable whether two opponents who are still excited and mad could present a case as well as a lawyer who is used to arguing rationally under these circumstances. It's hard to generalize on lawyer participation. It depends on the specific case being considered. I might advise my client not to be represented in a simple case. But if the client is really concerned, he'll have the lawyer there.

In the study previously mentioned, Mentschikoff looked at the use of lawyers both in the self-contained trade-group arbitrations and in tribunals conducted within the American Arbitration Association. As pointed out earlier, she found that attorney representation in trade association arbitration was rare. In investigating the reason for this phenomenon, she cites two principal arguments:

1. Lawyers did not understand the business usages and practices that were typically involved in adjudicating the dispute and therefore were not helpful.
2. Lawyers made the proceedings unduly technical and tended to create unnecessary delays.[13]

Mentschikoff's research also found that in the trade groups, a large amount of emphasis in deciding upon cases arbitrated is given to norms and standards peculiar to the trade in question.

Without the benefit of a firsthand knowledge of trade group arbitration

[11] *Ibid.*, p. 8.
[12] *Ibid.*, p. 5.
[13] *Mentschikoff*, op. cit., p. 859.

gathered through an extended period of observation, it is difficult to comment upon the validity of the criticisms recorded by Mentschikoff. Our own research, however, leads us to believe that the contrast in the actual methods and procedures of arbitration between the trade groups and those conducted by the American Arbitration Association affords a strong reason for the variance in the degree of lawyer participation.

Our questionnaires and interviews also indicated an historical desire of trade groups to keep close internal control over their members' disputes and their method of resolution. This desire has led the groups to set up their own arbitration procedures, to select arbitrators from their membership, and to discourage the opposing parties' representation by outside lawyers. Moreover, the repetitive and routine nature of the vast majority of trade group disputes has limited the need for legal counsel.

Soia Mentschikoff's research has thrown an interesting light upon the use of attorneys within the American Arbitration Association. Her finding, based on an analysis of records at the Association, was that the use of legal representation in the tribunal significantly lengthened the duration of the cases. It could be argued, as she recognizes, that because the use of legal representation increased with the amount of money involved in the cases, the relationship between legal representation and the cases' duration was coincidental. However, Mentschikoff's observation is that the relationship was more direct: "Personal observation at the Association leads me to the reluctant conclusion that in the great majority of the cases observed, lawyer participation not only failed to facilitate decision, but was so inadequate as to materially lengthen and complicate the presentation of the cases."[14]

This conclusion raises some strong questions as to the sagacity of advocating legal representation. We were interested not only in the validity of Soia Mentschikoff's conclusion but also in determining possible reasons for it. As a part of our research, the authors sent out 230 questionnaires to arbitrators of commercial cases in the American Arbitration Association. The responses which were received (130) tended to support Soia Mentschikoff's statements.

Our tentative conclusion, reached as a result of the arbitrator questionnaire, is that the lawyer's capabilities, as stressed by the American Arbitration Association, can be used most effectively in presenting a case in commercial arbitration. A less than adequate level of preparation, however, combined with a reluctance to abandon practices condoned and valued in the courtroom, have curtailed the effectiveness of his capabilities.

[14] *Ibid.*, p. 859.

In the arbitrator questionnaire, we queried: "What factors do you feel are critical to a winning presentation by a party?" The response to this question (followed by the number of respondents) can be broken down as follows: facts, supported by documents, testimony, and so forth, 44; degree of preparation, especially in customs of trade, 38; a clear, concise presentation, 36; attitude of the parties, 11; appearance of honesty in parties and witnesses, 9. The amount of importance attached by the arbitrators' response to the development of facts, careful preparation, and a clear, logical presentation would seem to support the American Arbitration Association's contention that many of a lawyer's abilities are required to the same extent in arbitration as in litigation. One could also contend that the importance attached to the attitude and appearance of the parties and witnesses by the arbitrators is not unlike the importance which would be attached to such things by a jury. In light of this, why does Mentschikoff's conclusion appear to have merit?

Part of the answer appears to be that many lawyers simply have not done an adequate job of preparing their cases to make a convincing presentation. In answer to the question referred to above (What factors do you feel are critical for a winning presentation by a party?), we drew comments pointing in this direction. One arbitrator stated, "On many occasions one of the attorneys has not been familiar with the industry in question." Another arbitrator, who has a legal background and has heard 20 cases in the past 10 years, stated rather flatly, "Most lawyers *not* prepared." (Emphasis his.)

These feelings were supported by answers to another question posed: What are the present weaknesses of commercial arbitration? Here again, lack of preparation by counsel was the most frequently cited factor.

Just why this condition exists is a question that perplexes the authors. We can only raise some tentative hypotheses in the way of an answer. One, that lawyers view commercial arbitration as a second-rate forum whose relative informality negates the need for as meticulous preparation as in court. Two, that lawyers do not feel that arbitrators will be as demanding of a tightly woven case as would be a judge. Three, that as the amount at stake in arbitration is often less than in litigation, the amount of preparation lawyers feel is warranted is correspondingly less. Four, that the relatively short period between the dispute and hearing sometimes present in the arbitration process precludes adequate preparation, especially for the party upon whom the notice to arbitrate is served. Five, that the parties in arbitration are not being represented by the most talented lawyers available.

A second factor curtailing the lawyer's effectiveness in the arbitration tribunal appears to be a failure to adapt to the situation of the tribunal, as opposed to the courtroom. The importance of doing this is increased by the fact that of the cases conducted by the American Arbitration Association, only 20 percent are heard by arbitrators with a legal background. In front of a lawyer arbitrator, the adaptation might not be as important, as indicated by the following excerpt from a paper on commercial arbitration by Charles Horowitz:

> My own experience in acting as an arbitrator is probably not typical by reason of the fact that rules of law were required in one case and heavily relied upon in another. However, my experience does indicate that to a lawyer, at least, acting as an arbitrator, a mode of presentation with which he is most likely to be familiar and which is most likely to be acceptable to him is a presentation which follows the methods used in court trials. When the presentation departs from procedures with which the lawyer member of the arbitration board is familiar, such a member is called upon to evaluate the departures and sometimes to draw adverse inferences from such departures.[15]

As Horowitz points out, however, his experience is based upon two cases which involved questions of law. Our research has shown that at least in those cases heard at the American Arbitration Association, less than 25 percent do involve questions of law. This finding, combined with the relative predominance of nonlawyer arbitrators, diminishes the importance of following many of the court procedures in presenting a successful case.

The comments received from the arbitrators in answer to our questionnaire stressed that a lawyer's presentation may suffer from being overly technical in a legal sense. For example, in answer to the question referred to earlier (What factors do you feel are critical to a winning presentation by a party?), one respondent who has arbitrated over 200 cases in the past 14 years stated, "Don't let the lawyers get too legal." Another arbitrator, while upholding the importance of preparation and a clear and well-organized presentation, stated that courtroom tactics were much less important because of the informality of the proceedings. A third respondent emphasized the importance of a "good preparation presented concisely" by underlining "concisely" and adding the parenthetical remark that "Lawyers love to talk."

Bearing upon this same point were answers provided by arbitrators to

---

[15] Charles Horowitz, "Some Observations on Commercial Arbitration." Address to the Seattle Bar, September 1961.

this question: What are the present weaknesses of commercial arbitration? Representative answers to this question were:

- Failure of attorneys of contestants to understand the difference between an arbitration and a court proceeding.
- Resistance of lawyers to change.
- Too much tendency of lawyers to try to simulate a courtroom.
- Tendency of legal counsel to attempt to cloud issues with technical details especially when poorly prepared.
- Lack of experience of attorneys in arbitration practice and procedure.

These responses lead us to believe that for a lawyer to be really effective in representing a client in commercial arbitration, he must be well versed in the tribunals' procedures and aware of the differences therein from those of the courtroom. Perhaps the American Arbitration Association, in its desire to promote commercial arbitration to the legal community and win the lawyers' acceptance, has overstated the degree of similarity that arbitration shares with courtroom proceedings. A possible reason for the apparent failure of lawyers to adapt to the arbitration process might well be a lack of familiarity which only experience or more pragmatic education can bring.

Knowledge of and experience with commercial arbitration could be considered to be important determinants not only of how well the lawyer functions in a tribunal but also of whether he recommends the employment of an arbitration clause or settlement of a given dispute through the process in the first place. It is highly dubious that a lawyer will advise his client to enter an agreement, committing himself to the machinery for a quasi-legal process, without such a familiarity. Given the great extent to which the business manager relies upon counsel in the decision of how to handle current or future disputes, the legal community's knowledge of and experience with commercial arbitration is a significant factor in determining the process' future.

THE LAWYER'S FAMILIARITY WITH COMMERCIAL ARBITRATION

In our research, we sought to determine to what extent the legal community in this country is familiar with commercial arbitration. We found early in our study that a sound determination of this knowledge would be nearly impossible because of the subjectivity of such a rating. We cannot claim that our findings in this area were based upon a scientific sampling of the legal community. Rather, they are based upon interviews we held with lawyers, the response to a questionnaire sent to 170 law firms, and the answers to a second questionnaire addressed to the deans of 48 law schools in the United States. The strongest argument supporting the validity of our conclusion is the consistency of response from these three different sources.

Our interviews with lawyers indicated that there exists a relatively high degree of ignorance on the part of the legal community concerning commercial arbitration's procedures. The feeling most often expressed was that most lawyers have learned enough about the process to be able to distinguish its departures from courtroom procedure. In the eyes of a lawyer whose training and experience had led him to respect courtroom procedures, these distinguishing characteristics have, on the whole, appeared unfavorable. This initial impression has succeeded in causing a hesitation on the lawyer's part to argue "out of his element," where the tools of his trade are subordinated to more mundane and, in his eyes, inappropriate influences. The attorneys interviewed felt that the lawyer's reluctance to subject himself to a foreign proceeding has been a significant factor in slowing the evolution toward a more thorough acquaintance with the process.

As mentioned earlier, the authors sent a questionnaire on commercial arbitration to law firms throughout the United States. The firms selected were a sample of the larger firms practicing corporation law in the commercial centers of the country. The response to this questionnaire reinforced the impression gathered from our interviews.

Of the 170 law firms solicited, 80 replied to the questionnaire, and 19 declined to answer any of the questions because of a lack of experience or knowledge of the process. We feel, in light of the average size and type of practice represented by the firms polled, that this number of decliners is significant.

In the questionnaire, the following was asked: "Have you or your firm been engaged in commercial arbitration proceedings? If so, approximate number of cases per year." This question was answered by 57 lawyers; of them, 20 answered "No." Only six of the respondents indicated that they or their firm engaged in over ten cases per year. In answer to other questions, relating to various aspects of the process, an average of 20 to 25 percent of the respondents replied that the lack of experience with commercial arbitration prevented them from offering a meaningful response. Still others commented at the end of the questionnaire that their answers were based on opinion and secondhand knowledge rather than on actual experience.

As stated, we do not believe that our study in any way could be said to represent the entire spectrum of lawyers in the United States. However, we feel that the firms polled should be representative of that portion of the legal community that would have the closest contact with, and the most opportunities to apply, commercial arbitration. On the basis of our responses, we believe that many of the lawyers who are in a position to use commercial arbitration are disinclined to do so effectively at this time because of a lack of familiarity with the process.

Our research indicates that comparatively little is being done by law schools in the country to equip students with a fundamental knowledge of commercial arbitration. At the time of writing, the authors had received 30 responses from the deans of different law schools to a query on the extent to which commercial arbitration is included in the schools' curricula. In 15 of the 30 schools, no course is offered that deals with commercial arbitration. The deans of 13 schools replied that the process was dealt with in one or more courses, but in only two of these instances were more than one or two hours of the entire program devoted to it. The final two schools replied that commercial arbitration was not covered in class but that it was included in assigned reading in one or more courses.

A conclusion arrived at earlier was that a lawyer will be reluctant to recommend a commercial arbitration contractual clause or settlement to a client unless he is familiar with the process. If this is correct, our findings on the lawyer's lack of familiarity with commercial arbitration indicate that any growth of the process' use in the near future is unlikely to be stimulated by the legal community. Indeed, it appears that before such a growth occurs, there is no small amount of inertia to be overcome. Whether this can or will be accomplished will depend not only on the lawyer being supplied with compelling reasons why commercial arbitration should be more widely employed but also on the nature and strength of the lawyer's attitudes toward the process.

THE LAWYER'S ATTITUDE TOWARD COMMERCIAL ARBITRATION

The major reason for the lawyer questionnaire described in the preceding section was to determine the *current* opinion and attitude of the legal profession toward commercial arbitration. The response to this questionnaire forms the basis of our findings on the lawyer's attitude towards tangible and intangible aspects of the process. This basic input was supplemented by separate interviews with corporation lawyers and by articles in legal publications such as the law reviews.

Scrutiny of the lawyer's perception of arbitration is of significant importance as it can seriously affect commercial arbitration. It is obvious that stated negative opinions are injurious, but what is often overlooked is the fact that the parochial viewpoint which portrays commercial arbitration as a complete or almost complete panacea for business problems can also be harmful. This potential for harm is real.

Lawyers are all too familiar with the vagaries of human nature to accept *any* process as a cure-all leading always to equitable settlement of disputes. As a result, they have a tendency to be skeptical of a device for which such claims are made or implied. This in itself is clearly injurious to the practice of commercial arbitration. An equally serious danger lies in the response that such altruistic exclamations may evoke. One prominent attorney, the author of an articulate and biting criticism of commercial arbitration, said in an interview that he was prompted to write the article for precisely this reason. This man is well known and respected in his profession. His opinion is doubtless valued by his colleagues, and, given the general unfamiliarity lawyers have with arbitration, his critical article may in some cases stand as a lawyer's total research into the possibilities of commercial arbitration. Obviously, the results of such limited research would lead to a negative attitude.

This general unfamiliarity, even on the part of a lawyer who will investigate beyond one article, further underscores the danger inherent in the diversity of opinion concerning arbitration. Driven off by opponents of arbitration and made skeptical by its adherents, he is left in a quandary. There are, to be sure, occasional attempts to put the process in perspective. These are few and far between, however, and by the time one appears, the lawyer has frequently given up.

The solution to this problem, according to advocates of arbitration, is for the lawyer to become familiar with arbitration through practice. Such a solution does not appear to be realistic. Lawyers are a traditionally conservative group of people. It is doubtful that they can be persuaded to ply their trade in an alien environment unless *forced* to do so by a client or the circumstances of the case (for example, a prior contractual agreement to arbitrate). Consequently, in the majority of instances, education must precede actual involvement. Since voluntary involvement will not occur and since the conflicting opinions of arbitration remain an obstacle, it is difficult to see how the educational impetus needed to precipitate involvement can be provided.

A lawyer's frame of reference influences his perceptions of arbitration. These perceptions, both positive and negative, are consistently based upon evaluations of arbitration in relation to the courts. Things are either better than, or worse than, they are in litigation. The effects of negative opinion are damaging. But the danger implicit in a "just like the courts, only better" claim advanced by some proponents is more subtle. An example of such a claim can be seen in the prologue to an article appearing in *Business Management* in 1961: "You can settle business wrangles quickly, painlessly, and privately through commercial arbitration. It's much faster than the courts, usually far cheaper, and there's no danger of notoriety. . . ."[16] Taken together with the lawyer's tendency toward skepticism previously discussed, comparison with the courtroom seldom attracts lawyers to the process.

A lawyer has spent years training himself for practice in the courts. He is usually quite dedicated to the institution that symbolizes his profession. It has a long tradition ingrained in the very fibers of civilization, and in the lawyer's eyes it is one *raison d'etre* for the perpetuation of that civilization. The lawyer's perception of the judicial process has been eloquently stated by the late Dean Roscoe Pound of the Harvard Law School: "The history of civilization shows a movement toward a systematic application of politically organized society by trained magistrates according to a scientifically organized body of authoritative guides and grounds of decisions developed and applied by authoritative technique."[17] In view of such thoughts, it is not difficult to see why lawyers not only do not believe that there is something "just like the courts, only better," but resent the very idea that someone would say so.

Arbitration suffers from comparison with the courts for other reasons also. It isn't "just like the courts." In fact, its strongest points lie in those areas where it most widely differs from the courts. Arbitration and litigation have a similar goal. The proceedings of the two processes are somewhat alike, principally because the arbitration proceeding has been altered to accommodate the lawyer. In both processes, questions of fact pertaining to the dispute at hand are critical. The major difference is the framework within which these questions are examined. The rules of law which provide such a framework in litigation are at most a minor part of the arbitration process.

This difference presents some interesting implications. In both instances, knowledge of the facts concerning the dispute plus the ability to present these facts rationally are requisites. The difference lies in the rules of law which are such an important part of litigation and which are not in the

[16] "How to Settle Business Disputes Painlessly," *Business Management,* Vol. 21, No. 2 (November 1961), p. 60.
[17] Quoted in *The Arbitration Journal,* Vol. 15, No. 1 (1960), p. 35.

same degree present in arbitration. If we assume that the average business-man is capable of assembling, ordering, and presenting the facts in a dispute, then his need for a lawyer is critical only if he seeks litigation. This is true because it is the lawyer who is familiar with the rules of law involved and whose job is to utilize these rules to his client's advantage. In arbitration, a lawyer is necessary only to the extent similar rules exist.

Whether these rules and other legalistic trappings are present in arbitration proceedings to accommodate the adversary nature of counsel or because there is an unavoidable degree of conflict has been discussed. The fact remains that such trappings do exist, and they facilitate comparison of arbitration with litigation in spite of the important basic differences noted above.

It seems inevitable that lawyers will evaluate these tangible aspects of arbitration by comparison to court proceedings with which they are familiar. An interesting observation in this respect was made by Jerome D. Frank:

> Of course, psychiatrists point out that the human mind guides one's perceptions along the path of one's expectations. This was indicated by an experiment in which, by means of a stereopticon, different pictures were shown to the right and left eye simultaneously. When a baseball player and a bull fighter were shown, Americans tended to see the baseball player and Mexicans the bull fighter.[18]

Thus, is it not reasonable to assume that the lawyer when looking at arbitration "sees" the courtroom?

Rather than determining whether arbitration is more or less private than a court, it would seem more important to ask simply, is it private enough? Or is it critical that privacy exist at all? Instead of determining whether arbitrators have more or less legal knowledge and experience than judges, it might be more useful to investigate whether they have *enough* to settle the dispute before them; or indeed, whether they need any at all. Finally, it would seem more to the point to determine if it is important that arbitration decisions be predictable, rather than to determine that they were more or less predictable than court decisions.

Having postulated the importance of the lawyer's opinion to the future of commercial arbitration and illustrated the frame of reference used by the lawyer in stating these opinions, we can proceed to look at his perceptions and attitudes.

---

[18] Jerome D. Frank, "Breaking the Thought Barrier," *Psychiatry: Journal for the Study of Interpersonal Process,* Vol. 23, No. 3, August 1960.

Speed. The relative speed with which cases can be dispatched is often pointed to by proponents of commercial arbitration as one of the process' most valuable assets. This factor, they maintain, is made increasingly important by the crowded court dockets in the commercial centers of this country. Because this is held to be such an important factor, it is an appropriate one to use as a point of departure in describing the lawyer's attitudes toward commercial arbitration.

In our lawyer questionnaire, we asked this question: In comparison with litigation, how do you feel commercial arbitration stands with respect to speed? The response was broken down as follows:

Reply	*Number of Respondents*
Faster	39
Same	6
Slower	2

Few lawyers, as indicated by this response, dispute the fact that commercial arbitration can offer a means by which settlements are reached more quickly than by litigation.

However, the evidence we gathered on the importance of this factor to lawyers in deciding on whether to employ or recommend is less conclusive. In the same questionnaire, we queried: "In advising a client whether to insert an arbitration agreement into a contract, what weighting would you typically give [speed]?" The question was answered:

Weighting	*Number of Responses*
0%	12
25	4
50	12
75	16
100	9

Although in other parts of the questionnaire the factor of speed was mentioned more often than any other single factor as a strong point of the process, as an element in the decision to use arbitration it appears less important. Explanations for this response were solicited in our interviews with corporate lawyers.

In considering speed, the lawyers interviewed broke down the relevant time span into two periods: from the time of the dispute to the hearing, and from the beginning of the hearing to a final settlement. The general opinion of these lawyers was that if *both* parties are willing to arbitrate and desire a quick settlement, the two periods can be shorter with arbitration than with litigation. This they felt is particularly true in areas where the court dockets are crowded. Typically, after making this introductory statement, the lawyer would launch into a lengthy series of "howevers," of which the more frequently articulated will be described below.

If one party is not particularly desirous of speed and unwilling to cooperate to that end with the other, he can substantially lengthen the first part of this process in two ways. First, he can contest the validity of the arbitration agreement and demand litigation to compel him to arbitrate. Second, he can impede the process by delaying selection of arbitrator(s).

The lawyers interviewed were generally of the impression that in the case of litigation, although there is often a longer wait to get to the point of a hearing, that once at that point, it is reasonable to expect that the case will be dispatched in a few days. They did not have the same impression of arbitration, especially with a complicated case. Under this circumstance they felt that the hearing is often an extended fact-finding symposium that will require several meetings. Because of the outside commitments of part-time arbitrators the length of time between hearings can be significant, thus stretching the hearing and necessitating repetition in the presentations. Several of the lawyers expressed the opinion that often an arbitrator's inability or unwillingness to exclude the introduction of irrelevant testimony or other evidence materially lengthens the proceedings. Finally, there was the concern that the opposing parties would go to court to attempt to seek a review of the arbitrator's award.

The importance of speed, even when it can be obtained, was another consideration often addressed in our interviews. We gathered from many lawyers that a desire for speed more often stemmed from the business client rather than from the attorney. Two reasons were given for this. First, we gained the impression that few lawyers want to be rushed—that while it is the job of a businessman to act fast, this is not so in the case of a lawyer. Like the physician, a lawyer, in preparing his case, wishes to probe here and examine there, anxious to discover any hidden weaknesses and not overlook any potential strength. He likes to move in small steps and allow room to maneuveur. A move for a quick hearing can force a lawyer to settle for a less adequate level of preparation than would otherwise be true. Second, a shortened period from the dispute to the hearing can obviate a chance of an "out-of-court" settlement between the two parties. Finally, the lawyers interviewed felt that speed is not always of paramount importance in large commercial cases. They viewed speed in such cases as having the potential to interfere with effective settlement.

The foregoing is not to say that the lawyers with whom we met were oblivious of business conditions that could make the quick settlement of a dispute highly desirable. On the contrary, most of the lawyers cited conditions within the industries with which they were familiar that could make speed an important factor. The impression left with the authors, however, is that corporation lawyers do not regard the process' potential of offering a quick settlement to be a desirable quality, per se.

Economy. The majority of the lawyers polled felt that in comparison to litigation, commercial arbitration was less expensive to the client. Of the 47 lawyers who provided a specific response, 32 believed that commercial arbitration was less expensive, 10 were of the opinion that the costs to the client were about the same, and 5 felt that the process was more expensive to the client than litigation.

From comments on the questionnaire and from interviews, we found most lawyers expressing the belief that commercial arbitration's largest cost savings stemmed from the avoidance of pretrial activities. Because of this and the resultant increase in time to prepare briefs and so forth, the attorney's fee could be lower. However, all the attorneys interviewed were hesitant to generalize on the potential savings that commercial arbitration could afford their clients out of fear of the possibility that both sides would not always be willing to cooperate. The considerations we heard are well summarized and articulated by Charles Horowitz, who states that arbitration can be more economical than litigation provided that:

1. Parties forego procedural safeguards such as pretrial discovery procedures.
2. Expenses such as physical facilities and arbitrator fees and expenses are kept to a minimum. (In important cases, compensation payable to the arbitrator and clerk's expenses can be substantial.)
3. Admission of irrelevant and lengthy evidence is held to a minimum so as to keep the proceedings short.
4. Parties do not take advantage of certain states' statutes allowing them to resort to court prior to arbitration to contest the agreement's validity and scope or to demand review of the arbitrator's award through appeal.[19]

When there is some assurance that these conditions will prevail, most of the lawyers we saw expressed the opinion that commercial arbitration could afford significant cost savings to the client, especially in smaller cases. This feeling was supported by a questionnaire response in which economy was the third most frequently cited strong point of commercial arbitration.

---

[19] Charles Horowitz, *op. cit.*

Legal preparation. Earlier in this chapter, in looking at the role of the lawyer in the arbitration tribunal, we cited the current opinion of many arbitrators that legal counsel is often not adequately prepared. In addition, the answers we received concerning the cost of the process seemed to indicate that arbitration demanded less preparation on the part of the lawyer than litigation. We were surprised, therefore, at the response to this question posed to lawyers: In comparison to litigation, how do you feel commercial arbitration stands with respect to legal preparation required? The specific responses were:

Preparation	Number	Percent of Respondents
Same	28	58
Less	19	40
More	1	2

On the basis of our earlier discussion, we had anticipated that more lawyers would reply "less." This dichotomy could be explained by the uncertainty existing in the minds of many lawyers that a case brought to arbitration will be settled quickly without any resort to the courts. In our interviews with lawyers, the belief most generally expressed was that in simple arbitration cases, not complicated by court reviews, the demand for preparation was not as great as in litigation. Typical of the comments we heard on this point was the following:

> With small cases in commercial arbitration, you can get away with less preparation than in court due to the absence of pretrial activities. Also, due to arbitration's relative informality, you don't have to do the amount of work on things such as the admissibility of evidence. In court, you have to plan more elaborately beforehand just how the case is going to be developed.

However, at least one lawyer with whom we talked, who had considerable experience with arbitration, did not agree with the views expressed by the majority of other lawyers interviewed. It was his belief that comparable cases demand as much preparation in arbitration as in litigation. Perhaps it is this split in opinion over the amount or type of preparation required that has given rise to the complaints voiced by arbitrators.

Maintenance of goodwill. The relative informality of the arbitration proceedings as compared to court is often pointed to by proponents of commercial arbitration as an important factor in maintaining good relationships between opposing parties. Our research indicates that lawyers do regard this aspect of the process as being important when a continuing relationship between the parties exists.

The prevailing attitude of the lawyers interviewed was that arbitration proceedings could be less acrimonious than in court action but that this was completely dependent upon the parties' willingness to cooperate with and accommodate each other—when there was a *desire* to maintain good relations. Under other conditions, however, the lawyers felt that the lack of strict controls in the arbitration tribunal could serve to encourage increased antagonism between the two parties.

Aside from the relative informality of the proceedings, two additional characteristics of commercial arbitration were cited as contributing toward maintenance of goodwill. The first of these is that often both parties will respect the arbitrator's experience and ability to render an equitable decision by which both sides are willing to abide. The second is that a speedy settlement, more easily obtained in arbitration than in litigation, helps to preclude an escalation of ill feelings.

Although the lawyers polled recognized the positive influence that commercial arbitration could have upon maintaining good relations, it was not viewed as a particularly compelling reason for recommending arbitration. In our questionnaire, we asked the following question: "In advising a client whether to insert an arbitration agreement into a contract, what weighting would you typically give [goodwill]?" The response broke down as follows:

Weighting	Number of Respondents	Percent
0%	19	38
25	9	18
50	12	24
75	5	10
100	5	10

The relatively large number who felt that commercial arbitration's advantage over litigation in preserving goodwill was unimportant is noteworthy. At the same time, this goodwill aspect was one of the five most frequently mentioned strong points of the process. We conclude that lawyers feel that this is a definite strength of commercial arbitration but that the number of commercial cases in which this aspect could be utilized is not as great as advocates of the process would lead one to believe.

The arbitration procedure. The arbitration hearing is said to contain the elements of privacy, flexibility, and informality. Critics of arbitration claim that often these elements are not present. Occasionally, the presence or absence of these elements turned out to be of little importance to lawyers. An example of this attitude is reflected in the reactions of lawyers to the supposed advantage of privacy.

Privacy is not perceived by most lawyers as a critical factor in determining whether to arbitrate. Of the respondents to the lawyer questionnaire, 50 percent claimed that privacy was never an important factor in arbitration proceedings. Another 30 percent said it was an important factor in less than half the cases taken to commercial arbitration. There were some instances where lawyers claimed that threat of notoriety was a weapon potentially denied them if they arbitrated, but these instances were so infrequent as to be negligible.

The results of personal interviews with attorneys familiar with arbitration tended to substantiate the results of the questionnaire. While those interviewed qualified their replies somewhat, the general thought was that privacy was not an overriding factor. It was considered important in certain instances, especially when a professional or personal reputation was at stake as might be the case in disputes arising from employment contracts or in those involving professionals such as architects or engineers. The desirability of privacy would also be very important in cases where proprietary information, such as technical or trade secrets, might have to be revealed in the proceedings.

Privacy is usually desired for two reasons: either to preclude public knowledge that the proceedings are taking place or to prevent what transpires in the proceedings from becoming public information. If privacy is desired for the first of these reasons, then the advantage attributed to arbitration might not be important. In industries where arbitration is used quite extensively (the textile and spice trades, for example), the need for privacy is less since going to arbitration does not bear the onus it might where it is not such an accepted part of industry norms.

At the same time, privacy within certain industries is usually maintained when it is required. This is especially true when a strong trade association governs, for such an organization will obtain the cooperation which achieves privacy.

When a dispute arises between companies in different industries, however, both the desire and opportunity for privacy are likely to diminish. In the first place, contact between the parties is less frequent, and the desire to preserve a continuing relationship or to observe trade norms is not as strong. As a result, the arbitration could well end in court, either to contest arbitrability of the dispute or to review the decision. When this occurs, the existence of the proceedings becomes a matter of public record and privacy is no longer maintained.

If privacy is desired to prevent the testimony and evidence from becoming public, then arbitration provides an ideal vehicle. Since it is not in the public domain, there is no valid claim by anyone to the content of the proceedings. Moreover, since the arbitrators themselves are often aware of the commercial importance of guarding proprietary information and since there is no legal compulsion to submit material, it is possible to avoid entering such proprietary information into the proceedings. Thus privacy in this sense is doubly provided by arbitration.

Another feature of arbitration which provoked mixed reaction from members of the legal profession is the so-called inherent flexibility of the procedure. Predictably, it was looked on as both a blessing and a pox, but all were at least agreed on its existence. One respondent stated, "Informal discussion of differences is more likely to lead to settlement." On the other hand, another commented that the most serious drawback of arbitration was "lack of established procedures."

Acknowledgment of the existence of flexibility has important implications regardless of whether a particular attorney likes it. For one thing, it is a condition favorable for faster settlement of disputes, since the number of locations where arbitration can be held and the time and duration of hearings are theoretically unlimited. The proceedings themselves are not inhibited by adherence to strict procedure. As a general rule, with an experienced arbitrator and willing parties, the absence of formality enhances the chances for quicker settlement of disputes. The informal atmosphere might also have value to the extent it mutes the adversary aspects of the proceedings and thereby promotes cooperation and settlement.

The benefits derived from arbitration's informal proceedings are appreciated by relatively few attorneys. However, those who find flexibility and informality definite strong points of arbitration are typically those most experienced in arbitration cases. Respondents commenting favorably on this point represented law firms which averaged over ten commercial arbitration cases a year. (The overall average of the lawyers responding was slightly more than three per annum.) A respondent whose firm has had considerable experience with commercial arbitration stated that the process provides "a congenial atmosphere in which to give and take in reaching a solution of disputes."

Other lawyers, however, look upon the lack of established procedure as a significant drawback of arbitration. It is difficult to determine whether these lawyers decry the lack of formal procedure because they feel without it the facts of the dispute will not be adequately presented, or simply because they feel uncomfortable without it. One lawyer stated quite frankly in an interview that it was the latter. He maintained, however, that the discomfort was not the result of any feeling of inadequacy or awkwardness on the part of the attorney but simply a feeling that if the institutions of the courts were not present "less" justice would be obtained. Another lawyer stated, on perhaps a more realistic basis, that the "lack of aura of the prestigious form" hindered acceptance of arbitration by the legal fraternity.

There are some attorneys, on the other hand, who feel that the lack of formal procedure impedes presentation of facts and rational judgment. They feel that without form proceedings wander, get out of hand all too easily, and become susceptible to the introduction of mass irrelevance and the use of subterfuge if one counsel is so inclined.

Perhaps the most controversial aspect of the flexibility question from this standpoint is lack of set rules governing the admissibility of evidence. Of all the legalistic attributes lacking in arbitration this is the one which bears most heavily on the determination of the facts in a dispute. Consequently, it is not only a question of considerable concern to the legal profession but also one that quite seriously affects the arbitration process as a whole.

It would be difficult to define a typical lawyer's attitude toward the admissibility of evidence in arbitration proceedings. Statistically speaking, over 60 percent of those expressing an opinion on this aspect of arbitration felt the loose rules were a definite drawback. One respondent stated in this regard, "As a lawyer, I deplore the sloppy application of rules of evidence, but a sociologist might say a higher form of justice is actually dispensed thereby." Among the others replying, 25 percent felt the loose rules were a strong point, and the remainder felt that they were not a significant factor. Examples of the diametrically opposed opinions received were such comments as "chaotic" and "too loose," on the one hand, and "it is an escape from the burdensome rules of evidence used in courts" on the other.

One of the most significant aspects of this question is that in only one isolated instance were rules of evidence advocated for their own sake. (Every other comment was focused on the real or potential influence of rules of evidence in facilitating dispute settlements.) The concern was not that critical evidence would be excluded, but that it could well be overlooked in a record "cluttered with irrelevancies," as one respondent put it. The question then is not one of not enough evidence but of too much.

Those representing the opposite viewpoint feel that in many arbitration cases, there is much more than legal questions to be settled and that limits placed on the admissibility of evidence might impede the rendering of an equitable decision. They claim that the loose practice is "good in technical cases especially," and "in keeping with the basic principles of arbitration."

Fully half the responses received concerning the admissibility of evidence were qualified in some degree by reference to the arbitrator. Such comments as "depends on the arbitrator," "no problem, if there is confidence in the arbitrator," and "cannot be any limitations, other than arbitrator's discretion" indicate the degree to which lawyers feel the arbitrator, rather than the presence or absence of any rule, governs whether appropriate and sufficient evidence is entered. This goes beyond mere recognition of the fact that it is the arbitrator who has sole control over the admission of evidence. It implicitly states that this is not a drawback, *provided the arbitrator rationally, consciously, and independently* exercises this prerogative. Two lawyers, both familiar with and favorably disposed toward commercial arbitration, indicated during personal interviews that they were concerned with the manner in which the arbitrator handles evidence. One commented: "Commercial arbitration's lack of such rules [of evidence] in the hands of a poor arbitrator is not an advantage." The second attorney stated: "If objection is made to the introduction of evidence, the arbitrator may well decide to let the evidence in even though the evidence is neither pertinent nor material to the controversy. This action prolongs the hearing and increases the expense."

Laying the admissibility problem at the feet of the arbitrators seems to be a logical reaction, and one probably taken in good faith by the legal profession. The lack of set rules necessitates a high degree of discretion and positive control by those charged with governing the proceedings. Establishing arbitrator responsibility for the practical rules of evidence, however, solves only a portion of a much larger problem. Because of the nature of the disputes brought before arbitration, an arbitrator could satisfy court practice in his use of rules of evidence and still not properly settle the dispute. The lawyer's frame of reference is, naturally, the body of rules governing evidence admissibility in courts. His belief in the validity of these rules is justified. They have evolved over a long period of time and are cogent in the courtroom. They are ideal tools in the matters of law for which they have been patiently and carefully developed. Arguments supporting their use outside this context are open to question, however.

Lawyers are aware of the basic differences between arbitration and litigation and, when questioned, acknowledge that the difference is significant enough that a transfer of litigation's rules of evidence to arbitration is not desirable. As has been mentioned, however, current practice concerning admissibility of evidence was a common drawback of arbitration cited by lawyers questioned. As one respondent put it: "There should be a trend towards established judicial rules in this respect and less emphasis on the fact that in arbitration proceedings the 'formalities and technicalities' should be avoided."

The term "trend towards" is significant, for while many lawyers found fault with present practice concerning admissibility of evidence, no one commenting on the question recommended that courtroom rules of evidence be adopted. The most restrictive measure proposed was the adoption of the evidence rules used in administrative proceedings of Federal regulatory agencies. Otherwise, no formal rules were proposed, beyond one recommendation that a lawyer sit on the tribunal to rule on admissibility. For the most part, the attorneys responding stated simply that arbitrators use more discretion and be independent enough to avoid the "let it in, for whatever it's worth" syndrome. In short, lawyers do not appear to take issue with the concept of admissibility found in arbitration but only in the way that this concept is interpreted. In commenting on the practice, they generally associated its virtue or lack thereof with the arbitrator.

The arbitrator. The acceptance in concept but concern over the practice of arbitrators with relation to the admissibility of evidence is similar to what appears to be the lawyer's attitude toward arbitrators in general. Over 73 percent of the respondents to the lawyer questionnaire felt that technical expertise of the arbitrators was an important factor in the majority of cases. Technical expertise or special knowledge was a feature of arbitration mentioned quite frequently. Of all responses to the question "If you were to list three of commercial arbitration's strongest assets, what would they be?" 62 per cent listed arbitrator expertise. It would appear that the principle of the expert tribune, long hailed by the champions of arbitration, is accepted by the legal fraternity.

In reality, however, the expert tribune enjoys little of the acceptance extended to him in theory. Of the "serious drawbacks" of arbitration suggested by respondents to the questionnaire, 50 percent were related in one way or another to shortcomings of the arbitrator. Arbitrators were described as "prejudiced," "incompetent," and "tractable." According to some comments, they "have a tendency to compromise," are "susceptible to business or social pressure," and "can be easily controlled by either side by principles of law."

Not all of the replies were subjective in nature. Attorneys found fault with some of the mechanics involved in selecting the arbitrators. The most frequent drawbacks listed in this regard were: (1) difficulty in selecting or agreeing on arbitrators, and (2) the failure of the American Arbitration Association to screen prospective arbitrators adequately. This latter point was covered in a previous chapter of this book.

It is important to note that on the question of arbitrators the polarization of responses was not nearly as clearly defined as it was on other issues. The same respondent in many cases listed arbitrator expertise as an asset and some factor concerning the arbitrator as a serious drawback. Initial reaction to such an apparent dichotomy might be to suspect the lawyer's motives. One could speculate that the expert tribune theory is too logical for the lawyer to rebuke so he begrudgingly accepts it only to reject it by means of its practice. However, such does not appear to be the case. For if a lawyer were to opt for the removal of the technical expert, one might assume that it would be in favor of a legal expert. Yet only 10 percent of the "serious drawbacks" submitted, or in any way suggested, that lack of legal expertise was the key issue. The other 90 percent focused on more general characteristics, aptitudes, and practices.

The lawyer, while acknowledging the technical expertise of the arbitrator, does not wholly accept him for it. Since he is not a judge and does not automatically possess the traditional independence, sagacity, and dignity which is perceived as associated with the title, the arbitrator is open to criticism. He is not sheltered by professional and social courtesy as are judges. In addition, the judge is one of the lawyer's own and holds a position to which many lawyers aspire.

Selection of arbitrators has been treated extensively in earlier parts of this book. All that will be mentioned here are a few thoughts emanating from lawyers' comments on this point. Mentschikoff, in an article for the *Columbia Law Review,* stated:

> . . . this right to participate in and, in large measure, to control the selection of arbitrators affords persons using the arbitral process an enormous advantage over those using the courts, since in the courts, within narrow limits of tactical maneuvering, the parties have no say in the selection of the judge who will try the case.[20]

Attorneys questioned were not in full agreement on the "enormous advantage" to be gained from the selection of arbitrators. They claimed that an advantage was realized in trade groups long used to arbitration, where arbitrators had established reputations, or when the arbitrators or alter-

---

[20] Soia Mentschikoff, *op. cit.,* p. 863.

nates were specified in the contractual clause. Outside these circumstances, however, there was some skepticism over how great an advantage the selection of arbitrators presented.

One attorney stated that in litigation while you perhaps cannot pick and choose your judge, you know, or can find out, infinitely more about him and his past record than you can an arbitrator and can prepare your case accordingly. The abundance of commercial arbitrators made selection and investigation difficult. Commenting on this same point, another attorney claimed that polling all 90 members of his law firm was often necessary solely to identify three names on an American Arbitration Association panel.

From the lawyer's standpoint this points toward the need for a tighter cadre of more experienced arbitrators. By becoming more "judge-like," they would be professionally more palatable to the lawyers, and perhaps some of the ills which might justifiably be identified by attorneys as currently existing within the arbitrator corps could be eliminated. Indeed, within trade groups, notably the maritime and textile industries and the New York Stock Exchange, such a cadre exists.

The award. The arbitrator's major function is to render a decision, thereby effecting settlement of the dispute. The attitudes and opinions of lawyers concerning the arbitrators' decisions are largely based upon their reactions to commercial arbitration's *lack of precedent, absence of written opinion,* and to the *finality of arbitration awards.*

The first two of these factors are quite closely related, in that precedent does not exist primarily because opinions are not commonly written. As mentioned earlier, however, this is not universal. Respondents commented that there now are cases on the books in Ohio and that precedents can be cited and will be honored in Pennsylvania. Moreover, in some states—such as Ohio, New Jersey, and Michigan—written reports (not necessarily paralleling a court opinion in form, content, or purpose) are usually submitted.

While there is a relationship between precedent and written opinion, the purposes of the two elements are different in the minds of the lawyer. Precedent is used primarily as a basis for case preparation. Opinion is regarded as a tool for preventing irrational or capricious decisions or as a basis for appeal if it is alleged that such a decision has been rendered.

Precedent is not just a preparatory instrument as far as technical questions of law are concerned. It also is looked on as a vehicle facilitating prediction of results. It is apparently the latter use that is uppermost in the minds of lawyers. Lack of precedent was looked on as a negative aspect of arbitration by 55 percent of responding lawyers. Of those who expressed their reasons why, all but one cited the unpredictability engendered by the lack of precedent. In the words of one lawyer, "It makes it difficult to advise clients of possible action." No one stated that the lack of precedent for purposes of assisting in legal research was a problem, although one respondent did qualify this by saying precedent became more important when legal questions were involved.

Of more than passing interest in this regard is the fact that nearly 40 percent of those replying did not think lack of precedent was a significant issue. This is somewhat surprising in view of the fact that this aspect of arbitration has long been thought of as a primary reason why lawyers looked upon arbitration in a less than favorable manner. An explanation for this, suggested during personal interviews with lawyers who had arbitration experience, seems to be twofold. Theoretically, cases heard before an arbitrator principally concern questions of fact. According to one lawyer interviewed, precedent would be "inappropriate and confusing. Common sense, should in such cases be an adequate substitute for a knowledge of the law." Second, since most responding lawyers seek precedent primarily as a prediction device, their fears concerning its absence are soon allayed as they find that arbitrators "tend to feel bound by laws and by business codes so you can to an extent predict their inclinations."[21] The element of predictability which is missing for the most part in commercial arbitration is the opportunity to gain some information concerning the case of the opposing party. This would be gleaned from pretrial discovery proceedings in a court case.

The instrument on which precedent could be founded, the written opinion of the arbitrator, is also generally missing from arbitration proceedings. Of the lawyers questioned, 65 percent thought that this was a negative factor. The reasons for rejection of this principle fall, as mentioned, into two categories. First, there are those who believe that if written opinions were mandatory, they would serve as a deterrent to badly reasoned decisions. Respondents embracing this line of thinking feel that present practice "contributes to fuzzy thinking" on the part of the arbitrators and "encourages nonrational solutions and the rough justice of splitting differences." The second reason for wanting written opinions is to afford some basis for appealing an arbitration decision to the courts. Those who favor present practice, however, take an opposing stand at this point. They maintain that the risk that written opinions might provide a basis for appeal is

[21] Horowitz expressed an opposing view in his article; Horowitz, *op. cit.*

reason why they should not be encouraged. As one lawyer from Pennsylvania stated, "Because of the tendency to seek judicial review of awards, it seems desirable to avoid written opinions, especially conclusions of law, if awards are to have any finality." A doctrine laid down by the New York State Court of Appeals in 1902, and reiterated many times since, states that an arbitrator's award *cannot* be set aside for errors in judgment, either on questions of law or fact. An award can be set aside only if the arbitrator goes beyond his jurisdiction or is guilty of venality or misconduct. None of these conditions are likely to appear overtly in a written award if the arbitrator is the least bit intelligent. Furthermore, the necessity for written opinion would probably extend the time required to resolve a dispute and might discourage potential arbitrators from undertaking such work.

The attitude of the courts described above is significantly responsible for another characteristic of arbitration awards, their finality. Finality exists because there is no appellate machinery within the framework of arbitration itself, and the court will vacate the decision only upon the determination of gross error or misconduct described above. Curiously enough, in contrast to their attitudes toward lack of precedent and written opinion, lawyers polled favored the finality of arbitration awards by a 60-40 ratio. As one attorney put it, finality of awards is "difficult to take at times, but one of commercial arbitration's principal virtues." The opinion seemed to prevail that if arbitration is chosen as the method to settle disputes, finality, where supported by statutes, is one of the features being sought. This would imply that it plays a significant role in motivating counsel to arbitrate rather than go to the courts. In fact, where appeals have resulted from arbitration, there is some feeling that the proceedings serve no real purpose. A respondent commented on this point: "Our experience has been that they [arbitration awards] are not final enough. If arbitration is to be just a prelude to court proceedings, its usefulness is very limited." On the other hand some appear to have been driven away from arbitration because of finality. One person labeled it "disastrous" and went on to say, "This [finality] limits our use of arbitration to those cases that are uneconomic to handle by way of a lawsuit."

If, as was suggested at the beginning of this chapter, the lawyer is in the process of accommodating to the frame of reference in which business is conducted, then it is reasonable that he should not reject a method of dispute settlement that embodies finality of decision at the first level. Such finality might outrage the lawyer's concept of due process, but from the point of view of the businessman it may be economically sound when applied to the particular dispute in question.

Contractual clauses. Award finality is to many but one arm of a pincer which characterizes commercial arbitration as a menacing process. The other arm, similarly an inherent feature of the process buttressed by court decision, is the contractual arbitration clause. A clause specifying arbitration as a means of settling future disputes arising from a contract or breach thereof does not in itself provoke the distaste of the legal fraternity. Lawyers generally, however, are strongly opposed to the so-called general arbitration clause.[22]

According to its critics, the general arbitration clause has two basic drawbacks. In the first place, there is a feeling that any controversy or any breach relating to a contract might not realistically lend itself to settlement by arbitration. Secondly, because of its general nature, the arbitration clause might soon become "boiler plate." As a result, contract signatories could unwittingly become party to undesired arbitration, or ensuing arbitration might be imposed on the weaker of two parties having unequal bargaining power. In either case, the action is hardly voluntary. In a speech before the American Arbitration Association in early 1965, Associate Justice Goldberg stressed the necessity for arbitration to be voluntary and underscored the danger of the "boiler plate" clause.

> Voluntary arbitration must be voluntary in a real and genuine sense. There can be little concern that it is genuinely voluntary, when arbitration is agreed upon in collective bargaining between unions and employers possessing an equality, more or less, of bargaining power. The same is true of commercial arbitration between business concerns which enter into arbitration agreements knowingly and advisedly. The situation may be different, however, where an arbitration clause appears as "boiler plate" in an installment sales contract, a lease or other document where bargaining power may be unequal.[23]

Whitney North Seymour, former President of the American Bar Association and a strong proponent of arbitration, states with regard to this: "Lawyers should be able to recognize issues which are best excluded from coverage of arbitration clauses, opposed to those which turn on questions of fact or settled questions of law."[24] If this is the case, it is difficult to

[22] "Arbitration: Any controversy or claim arising out of or relating to this contract, or the breach thereof, shall be settled by arbitration in accordance with the Rules of the American Arbitration Association; and judgment upon the award rendered by the arbitrators may be entered in any Court having jurisdiction thereof." American Arbitration Association, *Commercial Arbitration Rules of the American Arbitration Association,* p. 2.
[23] Associate Justice Goldberg, Speech before the American Arbitration Association, New York, March 17, 1965.
[24] "How to Settle Business Disputes Painlessly," *op. cit.,* p. 63.

see how a clause committing both parties to arbitrate *all* disputes can be justified. The answer to this question is often offered in rebuttal to the second alleged drawback of the general clause. Those who favor its use state that if the clause is not of a universal nature, then litigation to contest arbitrability will become rampant. Moreover, if a dispute is taken to court for a jurisdictional ruling, proponents are concerned that the court will rule against use of arbitration unless the clause is general in nature. Therefore, those who favor the general clause see the end result under these conditions as chaotic—leading to litigation in almost all cases and foreclosing the use of arbitration.

The hypothesis does have historical basis. Soon after the passage of the New York Arbitration Act in 1920, a significant proportion of arbitration cases were brought to court to contest arbitrability. A series of extremely narrow interpretive decisions, often referred to as the Draft Act rulings, were handed down. These rulings so severely interpreted arbitrators' jurisdiction, as defined in specific clauses, as to prompt adoption and promotion of the general clause.[25] The argument still rages as to whether these decisions were prompted by jealousy of arbitration or by a sincere belief that arbitration was not in the public interest.

Regardless of the motives behind this somewhat negative attitude toward arbitration, there is every indication that it has undergone substantial change in the last 40 years. The pressures of crowded court calendars plus increasing evidence that arbitration is a valuable process have prompted many members of the bench to advocate its use. More importantly, recent court decisions have given unqualified sanction to the powers of the arbitrator. This trend in both official and unofficial attitude could well mean that the previously perceived dangers of a specific arbitration clause are not as great as they once were. On the other hand, Justice Goldberg's comments, often echoed by other jurists and members of the legal profession, could indicate a growing disenchantment with the general clause.

Given that the courts will equitably interpret arbitration clauses, the possibility still remains that specific clauses will present more of a temptation to take the dispute to court on grounds of arbitrability or finality. Thus the first part of the problem has not been solved. Even with a general clause, however, a contentious attorney can, and often does, challenge these points. If a party is determined to bring arbitration to the courts, he will do so. Thus it would not appear that many more cases would be taken

[25] See Phillip D. Phillips, "The Paradox in Arbitration Law: Compulsion as Applied to a Voluntary Proceeding," 46 *Harvard Law Review* 1258 (1933).

to court as a delaying or agitating tactic than happens now. The other occasion for contesting arbitrability, a genuine question as to whether the dispute can realistically be arbitrated, perhaps should go to court. Chances are the court will refer even this question to the arbitrators,[26] and if not, there is no longer any reason to believe their ruling would be capriciously against arbitration.

In view of the foregoing, there does not seem sufficient justification for continued advocation of the use of a general arbitration clause. Such a stand appears dated, and the drawbacks are manifold. First, as has been indicated by Seymour, there are limits to the practicality of arbitration. Second, in addition to the real dangers of the general clause from a practical standpoint, it presents an aura of coercion which is unattractive. As one lawyer put it, "The prostituted use of arbitration, by applying the so-called general clause, is one of the process' greatest weaknesses."

The general clause is not only an awkward and inhibiting feature of arbitration in the eyes of the lawyer, it also makes it many more enemies than friends. Unlike the other arm of the pincer, finality of award, it does not appear to have valid justification. It would seem under the circumstances that the use of more explicit arbitration clauses adopted, in the words of Justice Goldberg, "knowingly and advisedly" should make arbitration more workable, tend in the long run to keep it out of the courts, make it truly voluntary, and reduce what is apparently a substantial barrier to its acceptance by lawyers.

LAWYER'S VIEW AND KNOWLEDGE OF OTHER INFLUENCES

Despite what we detected as a lack of widespread familiarity with the process itself, the lawyers polled appeared to be well versed in those of their state's statutes which applied to commercial arbitration. With one exception, all of our respondents answered the question "Are your state's statutes favorable to commercial arbitration?" Many elaborated on this question by referring to the specific statutes applicable and pointed out what they felt to be the most important aspects of those statutes. A large number of attorneys also called our attention to relevant cases heard in their state's courts which have precedent value in determining the applicability and the enforceability of arbitration agreements and awards. The responding lawyers regarded their state's statutes as generally conducive

---

[26] *United Steelworkers of America vs. Warrior and Gulf Navigation Co.* 363 U.S. 574 (1960); *Robert Lawrence Co., Inc. vs. Devonshire Fabrics, Inc.,* 271 F.2d 402 (Second Circ. 1959).

to arbitration. In the cases where this was not true, they displayed a knowledge of why this was not so. This response indicated to the authors that at least in the case of those lawyers polled, any reluctance to employ arbitration is in no way attributable to an ignorance of the applicable statutes controlling its use.

Outside of New York and Pennsylvania, few of the responding lawyers felt that commercial arbitration was used extensively. To the question "To what extent is commercial arbitration used in your geographic area?" approximately two-thirds of the lawyers replied, "Very little." Most of the lawyers responding from the Northeast, Midwest, and West Coast expressed the belief, however, that the use of commercial arbitration is increasing. No lawyer saw its usage as decreasing. The majority of those attorneys from the Southeast, South, and Southwest, as well as several in the Midwest, felt that the use of commercial arbitration was neither increasing nor decreasing. Assuming that this response is representative of the views of the majority of the corporation lawyers, our guess would be that the need felt by corporation lawyers to become more familiar with commercial arbitration varies with different areas of the country. Supporting this is the fact that typically those lawyers who indicated a desire to see the results of our research were from those areas in which the use of commercial arbitration was seen as increasing.

In an attempt to determine whether commercial arbitration is more attractive to the lawyer or to the businessman, and which is more actively encouraging its use, we asked lawyers, "Is [commercial arbitration] advocated to a greater extent by the legal profession, the business community, or equally by both?" Forty-four lawyers responded thus:

Party	Number of Respondents
Legal profession	3
Business community	20
Both	6
Neither very much	15

As can be seen, in those cases in which lawyers feel that the process is being advocated, it is largely the business community that is the encouraging party. One might interpret from this response that much past growth in the use of commercial arbitration has resulted from the acceptance and enthusiasm of the businessman. Even if such an interpretation were correct, however, one should bear in mind the reliance of the business manager upon counsel in deciding how present or future disputes are to be handled. Regardless of the appeal that commercial arbitration may hold for the business manager, it appears that increased use of the process will be contingent upon its acceptance by the corporation lawyer.

A SUMMARY OF LAWYERS' VIEWS

Thus far we have discussed lawyers' perceptions of several individual facets of commercial arbitration. To distill these opinions and to focus on the lawyer's major concerns, we asked attorneys for their view of arbitration's strongest assets and most serious drawbacks. In addition, we solicited ideas on what modifications would make the process more valuable and where commercial arbitration can be most gainfully employed.

In the responses, no single factor emerged as the governing influence on the lawyer's decision of whether to arbitrate. From the comments, however, it is possible to detect an order of priority in the various characteristics of the process as they influence the lawyer's decision.

The strong points of commercial arbitration perceived by our respondents fell into three major groups of importance. Of the 20 different strong points suggested, the three most frequently submitted accounted for 65 percent of all replies. These were speed, arbitrator's expertise, and economy, in that order. The second group included the finality of the arbitrator's award, maintenance of goodwill, privacy, and informality. This grouping represented 25 percent of total replies. Thirteen other factors were evenly distributed within the remaining 10 percent.

To serve as a summary of the most serious objections held by the legal community to commercial arbitration, we asked the following: What do you feel to be commercial arbitration's most serious drawbacks? Of 32 different factors cited by the respondents, 14 were concerned with alleged shortcomings of arbitrators. When these are considered to form one category of objection, they represented nearly 40 percent of all responses. Other frequently mentioned drawbacks were the absence of established procedure, the inability to appeal awards, and the process' disregard for established rules of evidence. These factors, combined with the first category, constituted over 80 percent of those mentioned. This response indicated to the authors that the lawyer's current view of the abilities of arbitrators selected could serve as a serious impediment to the growth of commercial arbitration.

As one would expect, over 80 percent of the proposals submitted by lawyers for modifying the proceedings dealt with one or more of the drawbacks frequently mentioned. In most cases, the modifications proposed would bring more courtroom practices into the arbitration process. The only exceptions to this were those suggestions dealing with rules of evidence. As was mentioned earlier, no one advocated complete transfer of courtroom rules.

To summarize lawyers' views on the applicability of commercial arbitration, we asked the following question: What sort of cases are best suited to resolution through commercial arbitration? To this question we received a number of varied answers, in which several characteristics were often mentioned.

Most commonly mentioned were cases involving questions of fact, those in which factual issues lent themselves to the expertise of the arbitrators. On the whole, the lawyers responding felt that when the important issues of the case were those of law, rather than fact, the case had little place in arbitration. Cases in which commercial standards of performance and determinations of quality were important were often mentioned as being suitable for resolution through arbitration. Here two specific types of cases of which the lawyers often spoke were complex technical disputes and construction contracts involving language interpretation, or those in which elements of performance could not be defined immediately.

The responding lawyers indicated that where there is a continuing relationship between parties, when the maintenance of goodwill is important, and when there is a reasonable assurance that both sides will desire a quick settlement, commercial arbitration can offer a definite advantage over litigation. They felt that this was true also when privacy of the proceedings is important to maintain the reputation of the parties, although the relative occurrence of such circumstances was not held to be frequent.

Despite the opinion of several attorneys to the contrary, the majority of the lawyers believed that the size of the case should be an important determinant of whether to consider arbitration. It was often held that when the amount involved in the case was under $20,000 to $30,000, the cost of litigation is prohibitive.

Finally, in areas where foreign trade is commonplace, a large number of lawyers called our attention to the desirability of commercial arbitration clauses in international contracts. From the lawyer's standpoint, the principal feature cited was that this application of arbitration provided a defense against a client's being subjected to the jurisdiction of foreign countries.

* * *

In this chapter, we have been concerned with the relationship between the modern corporation lawyer and commercial arbitration. We have traced the growing importance of the lawyer's role in the business world and the extent to which his counsel is depended upon by the business manager. It was our finding that the lawyer is and will continue to be a governing figure in the decision of how business disputes are to be settled.

Within the commercial arbitration tribunal itself, however, the lawyer's position is less secure. Legal representation is encouraged by the American Arbitration Association and, at the same time, discouraged by numerous trade associations. Although a lawyer's training would seem to well equip him to present a case effectively in arbitration tribunals, many arbitrators have noted that inadequate preparation and a reluctance to abandon courtroom procedures have often prevented such an effectiveness from being realized.

Our research indicated that there is a widespread lack of familiarity of commercial arbitration's procedures on the part of the corporation lawyer. This lack of familiarity was seen as precluding the use of commercial arbitration by lawyers who might otherwise be in a position to utilize its strengths.

The lawyer's attitude toward commercial arbitration is often colored by a comparison with litigation. Due to the lawyer's typical respect for established court procedures, this comparison often results in resistance to many aspects of the arbitration process. This resistance has been increased by a skepticism toward claims made by proponents of the process who have overstated its similarity to court procedures and its ability to settle a wide variety of business disputes painlessly. In general, however, the lawyers polled displayed an appreciation for business conditions under which commercial arbitration can be effectively utilized. A number of their criticisms of the process are based upon perceived shortcomings of presiding arbitrators rather than upon commercial arbitration's procedural aspects. Lawyers were often of the opinion that commercial arbitration offers its greatest advantages when both parties are willing to arbitrate but that under other conditions the supposed advantages fall by the wayside. For this reason, the general arbitration clause which can lead away from voluntary decisions to arbitrate was frowned upon by many of the lawyers polled.

CHAPTER V

THE STATUTES, COURTS, AND COMMERCIAL ARBITRATION •

ALTHOUGH COMMERCIAL ARBITRATION is considered to be a businessman's dispute-settling process, it exists within a legal environment. The previous chapter explored the influence of individual lawyers on commercial arbitration. In this chapter we will examine the influence of two other aspects within the legal environment: the statutes governing arbitration and the congestion existing in courts today.

THE STATUTES AND COMMERCIAL ARBITRATION

The effectiveness of commercial arbitration is dependent on two factors: the desire of the parties to reach a settlement through arbitration rather than through litigation and the recognition and support given to arbitration in state statutes. It is the latter which lends force to arbitration as a dispute-solving process.

Arbitration, in most cases, is initiated by one party and is based on a prior agreement to arbitrate. The statute gives the force of law to this agreement and insures the enforceability of the subsequent award. The manner in which this is accomplished differs from state to state, and it is therefore necessary to contrast arbitration governed by a so-called "modern" statute with arbitration conducted under common law.

There is a striking difference between arbitration as governed by a specific modern arbitration statute and arbitration which relies on common law. The existence of a modern statute provides the only public environment (excluding that which exists within private associations) in which arbitration can become a viable dispute-settling mechanism. Under common law, a prior agreement to arbitrate is not enforceable.[1] A party which

---

[1] There have been two notable exceptions to this general statement where agreements to arbitrate were validated even though no state statute existed. See L. L. Fuller and R. Broucher, *Basic Contract Law* (St. Paul: West Publishing Co., 1964), p. 83.

agrees to arbitrate can withdraw from the arbitration at any time prior to the award. (But all states, under common law, will enforce an agreement to arbitrate that was created after the dispute. The volume of such agreements, however, is low.) After such a withdrawal, the only recourse for the party is litigation. This delays settlement of the dispute and vitiates one of the principal advantages of arbitration.

Twenty-one states have initiated modern arbitration statutes. These states are Arizona, California, Connecticut, Florida, Hawaii, Illinois, Louisiana, Maryland, Massachusetts, Michigan, Minnesota, New Hampshire, New Jersey, New York, Ohio, Oregon, Pennsylvania, Rhode Island, Washington, Wisconsin, and Wyoming.[2] One should note that these states contain most of the commercial activity in the United States and represent the areas where the greatest volume of litigation is conducted. Certain elements common to these statutes make arbitration effective.[3]

First, an effective agreement to arbitrate future issues must be enforceable and irrevocable. The law by which this is accomplished should be simply constructed, clearly worded, and include a minimum of technical legal requirements. The intent of such a section is to void the previous common-law rulings that agreements to arbitrate future disputes were unenforceable. Second, the statute should provide simple procedures for judicial recognition of the existence of the agreement and define the scope of arbitrability.

Third, the statute should protect the existence of the arbitration by explicitly directing that any court action concerning the issue being arbitrated be stayed until the arbitration is completed.

Fourth, the procedural details of the hearing should be included in the statute to indicate authority to appoint arbitrators, the number of arbitrators, the selection of the site, and details concerning expenses.

Fifth, the statute should lay down procedures and time limits for actions following the completion of the arbitration. This would include parameters for presenting the award, the form of the award, details for handling disputes over awards, modifying errors, and enforcement of the award.

The appeal provisions of most statutes limit court review of the arbitrator's decision to procedural issues involving fraud, miscalculations, overextension of authority, prejudice caused by misconduct of the arbi-

---

[2] Texas, Maine, and Oklahoma are contemplating changes in the structure of their laws to permit greater usage of arbitration. In addition evidence of increasing concern over arbitration can be seen in the recent revisions to the statutes of New York and California.

[3] See J. C. Dougherty and D. Graf, "Should Texas Revise Its Arbitration Statutes?" *Texas Law Review*, Vol. 41 (December 1962).

trator, and refusal to hear evidence. Thus it should be noted that judicial review is not over matters of substance but solely over procedures. It has been the intent of the statutes to limit court intervention and give substantial power to the arbitrator. (See Judge Andrew's opinion in *Fudicar* contained in Chapter II.)

In summary, an effective statute should facilitate the settlement of a commercial dispute in a manner that recognizes the original desires of the participants at the time the arbitration agreement is written.

COURT CONGESTION AND COMMERCIAL ARBITRATION

There has been a substantial increase in the use of commercial arbitration in recent years. Its increasing popularity, in part due to the aggressive work of the American Arbitration Association, has primarily been the result of the efficient and speedy handling of disputes afforded by the process. Our discussion of the lawyers' views of arbitration in the last chapter indicated that speed was one of the most significant factors influencing their decision to go to arbitration. *The Wall Street Journal* commented: "Arbitration has been used for many years in labor disputes, but now the increasing congestion in courts is channeling a rising number of non-labor cases to these referees."[4] We will note the crowded conditions of courts in this country today and then turn our attention to the impact that this is likely to have upon commercial arbitration.

The Federal and state judicial systems have been placed under substantial pressure by increasing workloads. A particularly heavy strain has been placed on courts serving the large urban centers. Chief Justice Warren has expressed concern over this situation:

> . . . the delay and the choking congestion in Federal courts today have created a crucial problem for constitutional government in the United States . . . . it is compromising the quality of justice available to the individual citizen and, in so doing, it leaves vulnerable throughout the world the reputation of the United States. . . .[5]

Court delay and its causes present a tremendously complex problem, a thorough examination of which is beyond the scope of this book. A number of possible causes for this condition have been brought to the attention of the authors in the course of the study.

The automobile has been pinpointed as one of the biggest problems

---

[4] *The Wall Street Journal,* May 21, 1961.
[5] Earl Warren, "Delay and Congestion in Courts," *42 Journal of American Judicature Society* 6, 6-7, (1958).

facing the New York State courts: "The conclusions are inescapable that automobiles are the principal source of litigation in the state, that they are the primary cause of delay in courts, particularly in large urban areas, and that they will continue to be so."[6] In support of this statement, the state was able to correlate the areas of court congestion with the areas having the highest accident rates. In 1963, personal injury cases accounted for 45 percent of the cases on the calendars of New York.[7]

This situation is not restricted to New York State. It has been estimated that in 1964, 60 to 70 percent of the total filings in the Minneapolis-St. Paul metropolitan counties and 45 percent of the Los Angeles Superior Court cases were personal injury cases. The problem is not a temporary one. Each year the total number of automobile registrations increases throughout the United States. As the highway population increases, increased personal injury load on the courts is inevitable.

A second factor causing court delay is the increase of population, particularly in urban areas. This growth has been accompanied by a greater use of litigation on a per capita basis. In Rhode Island's Kent County, a survey shows that over a 30-year period the population increased 128 percent and the number of cases filed increased 289 percent. If our more mobile population is indeed employing litigation at an accelerating rate, it appears that the problems facing our court planners will become more aggravated. The state court system of New Mexico, for example, faces a projected 25 percent increase in the state's population over a five-year period.

A factor in some areas has been the presence of a backlog which has existed since the 1920's. The early existence of delay is illustrated by a 1927 complaint: "The first defect in the administration of justice and one which has done most to lessen respect of people for justice and for its administration is what is commonly called the law's delays." In 1923, New York had 26,000 cases pending, an increase over a six-year period of 18,000 cases.[8] Backlogs from this period have been pushed forward through the years.

Finally, the lack of judges, facilities, and effective procedures for establishing court schedules, which are dependent upon the allocation of public funds, have contributed to the present congestion of courts.

---

[6] *1964 Report of the Senate Judiciary Committee,* State of New York, Legislative Document #44, December 15, 1964, p. 21.
[7] *1964 Report of the Senate Judiciary Committee, op. cit.,* p. 21.
[8] See Daniel Bloomfield (ed.), *Selected Articles on Commercial Arbitration* (New York: H. W. Wilson Co., 1927), p. 23.

Data gathered in our research on court congestion indicates that an individual going to trial (without a jury) in heavily populated areas of this country can expect to wait about 9-16 months before his case is tried. (See Exhibit 1.) A rough median of this period is 14 months. Jury trials in most cases require an even longer wait.

A sampling of current court delay indicates varying degrees of congestion in large urban areas throughout the United States. The average waiting periods in the cities of Seattle and Portland are about eight months. In other cities such as St. Paul, the wait is currently averaging 29 months, while the delays in metropolitan Detroit and Cleveland are 13.4 and 26 months respectively. Pittsburgh currently averages a 24-month wait after recently achieving a remarkable reduction from a 42-month delay.[9] California courts are showing the strain of servicing their growing population as nonjury trials involve a delay of 18 months in Los Angeles and 22 months in San Francisco. Rapidly growing areas such as San Jose now face an 18-month wait.

In all but one of the counties encompassing New York City, commercial cases are separated from other cases and placed on separate calendars.[10] As a result, commercial disputes can get to trial on the average of somewhat less than six months. In these counties, the waiting period ranges from two to thirteen months. This means that the businessman in New York City can get these disputes handled in court more rapidly than in the other major population centers. On the other hand, the personal injury calendar of all the courts within New York City is averaging a 42-month delay, with the individual counties averaging 33-50 months. If these calendars in New York were combined, the delay would be exceedingly long for all involved.

When one relates the magnitude of the growing delays in the major population centers to the causes of these delays, the possibility of getting quick and efficient settlement under present and anticipated conditions seems more and more remote. This is illustrated by the difficulty of the U.S. District Courts in meeting trial demands. The number of civil cases filed, terminated, and pending as of June 30 for fiscal years 1960 through 1964 are shown in Exhibit 2. Even though courts are handling an increased number of cases each year, they have been unable to keep pace with the increased number of filings.

[9] See "First Semi-Annual Report—The Court of Common Pleas of Allegheny County," *Pittsburgh Legal Journal,* July 30, 1964.
[10] *1964 Report of the Senate Judiciary, op. cit.,* p. 19.

MEASUREMENT OF STATE COURT DELAY

As an indication of the amount of court delay currently existing in the United States, the authors sampled relevant information from several states. The measurement of delay in court proceedings is difficult because different states and organizations follow slightly different procedures in defining and calculating a court's backlog.

A yardstick that appears useful for considering court delay is the median number of months that the parties have to wait to come to trial. However, this poses the problem of determining the most appropriate starting point. Some states measure from the time the plaintiff files, others from the filing of the answer. Since an answer is required before action can commence, we have used this method in our calculations. The following table illustrates the waiting periods existing in various states today.

Eastern States
New York:
    1. New York Supreme Court (1963 data)
        A. Six counties with tort time delay of 38-48 months.
        B. Four counties with tort time delay of 26-33 months.
        C. Eight counties with tort time delay of 13-21 months.
    2. County Courts outside of New York City*—
        Five counties with a tort time delay of 20-40 months
    3. Courts within New York City (June 30, 1964 data)
        A. Tort jury delay in 5 counties: 33-50 months
        B. Tort nonjury delay in 5 counties: 6-21 months
        C. Commercial jury delay* (excluding Bronx County): 3-13 months
        D. Commercial nonjury delay* (excluding Bronx County): 2-4 months
New Jersey*:
    The range of delays in the eight largest counties is 12-22 months.
Pennsylvania*:
    Allegheny County (Pittsburgh): 24 months

*Midwest States**
Minnesota:
    Minneapolis: 20 months
    St. Paul: 29 months
Michigan:
    Detroit: 13.4 months
Ohio:
    Cleveland: 26.2 months

*Far West States**
California:
    Los Angeles Superior Court (nonjury): 18 months
    Los Angeles Superior Courts (jury): 23.5 months
    San Francisco: 22 months
    San Diego: 11 months
    San Jose: 18 months
Hawaii:
    Honolulu: 17 months
Oregon:
    Equity: 7 months
    Law: 9 months
Washington:
    Seattle: Jury: 7.5 months
           Nonjury: 9.5 months

Sources:
    1. Latest available reports of State Courts' Administrators.
    2. Correspondence with Courts' Administrators.
    * 1963 and 1964 data.

EXHIBIT 1

TRIAL DEMANDS ON U.S. DISTRICT COURTS

	Filed		Terminated		Pending	
	Number	*% change over 1960*	*Number*	*% change over 1960*	*Number*	*% change over 1960*
1960	57,791	—	57,579	—	61,251	—
1961	58,293	0.9	55,416	−3.8	64,128	4.7
1962	61,836	7.0	57,996	0.7	67,968	11.0
1963	63,630	10.1	62,379	8.3	69,219	13.0
1964	66,930	15.8	63,954	11.1	72,195	17.9

Source: *Annual Report of the Director of the Administrative Office of the U.S. Courts*—1964 report, p. 29.

EXHIBIT 2

Under these circumstances, the relative speed that can be achieved by commercial arbitration is noteworthy. Of 1,134 cases sampled by the research department of the American Arbitration Association in the period 1958-1960, the median length of time from the initiation of an arbitration request to the hearing was three to four months.[11] When compared to the U.S. District Court (Southern District) of New York's median time to trial—29.3 months—for the same period, the significance of the figures becomes clear. (For current Federal Court statistics, see *Annual Report of the Director of the Administrative Office of the United States Courts,* 1964.) Only 38 arbitration cases, or about 3 percent were delayed over 12 months, while 157 of 167 nonjury cases were waiting for trial for more than a year.[12] While it must be recognized that many simple cases are sent to arbitration, it appears that arbitration can facilitate the quick handling of cases.

In view of this condition, the expanded use of arbitration or modification of court procedure to include certain aspects of arbitration seem to be practical relief measures. In fact, there are instances of relief remedies recently adopted by the courts which can be seen as gravitating toward arbitration. This is apparent in the use of a lawyer panel in pretrial procedures or the simplified procedures for the settlement of commercial disputes in New York Courts.

The latter procedure provides ". . . for what in effect is a judicial arbitration."[13] To speed up the proceedings, a single statement of claims, defenses, and requested relief is submitted to the court. This avoids the

[11] Albert S. Davis, Jr., "Patent Arbitration," *The Arbitration Journal,* Vol. 15, No. 3 (1960), p. 131.
[12] *Ibid.,* p. 131.
[13] "Recent Legislation," *Harvard Law Review,* Vol. 74 (1962), p. 1666.

time-consuming formal pleadings, and the signing of this combined statement also indicates the waiver of the right to jury trial. This is particularly important in New York State where delay in jury trials in many of the courts is exceedingly long.

Similar to arbitration, a prior agreement in a contract can specify that any dispute occurring as a result of the contract would be submitted under this procedure. This agreement is also enforceable by the courts and will stay any other court action until the completion of this action. The unique features of this action are the elimination of the rules of evidence (except under certain protective circumstances) and the court's right to seek the opinion of an impartial expert witness.

Another use of arbitration is seen in Pennsylvania, where the court can direct the use of compulsory arbitration before a panel of three lawyers to settle disputes involving sums up to $2,000. This procedure ". . . makes it possible for the immediate disposition of smaller claims . . . thus satisfying the need for prompt relief in such cases. By the same token, and working to the same end, the use of the act will free courts for speedier performance of other judicial functions."[14] After the institution of compulsory arbitration into the Municipal Court of Philadelphia, ". . . the major part of the Court's civil jurisdiction was directed to arbitration panels; in less than two years, delay fell sharply from between twenty-four and thirty-six months to between three and five months."[15] It has been estimated "that in the first twenty-two months the new procedure spared the courts not only some 1,996 full trials, but an additional 1,000 or so partial trials."[16] To date, the only application of compulsory arbitration is seen as being "in heavily congested courts of lesser jurisdiction."[17]

As described in Chapter I, effective use of arbitration has been made in the insurance area to avoid court delay. One insurance official announced that in addition to the time saved, his firm saved about $200,000 in a single year using this method of dispute settlement.[18]

On a wider scale, the use of commercial arbitration has been cited as an effective remedy for court congestion in the *1964 Report of the Senate Judiciary Committee* in the State of New York: "The present status of many of the calendars in [the Civil Court of the City of New York] requires

---

[14] Maurice Rosenberg and Myra Schubin, "Trial by Lawyer: Compulsory Arbitration of Small Claims in Pennsylvania," *The Harvard Law Review*, Vol. 75, p. 454.
[15] *Ibid.*, p. 458.
[16] *Ibid.*, p. 461.
[17] *Ibid.*, p. 471.
[18] See *The Wall Street Journal*, May 21, 1961.

immediate attention and action. Voluntary arbitration would undoubtedly have a beneficial effect on the calendars of this court."[19]

It appears that the strain on our court system will increase as our population grows and becomes more mechanized. In this environment, arbitration has a place, especially in those cases which deal with questions of fact. The increased utilization of commercial arbitration for commercial cases well suited for that process will leave increased judicial time to handle the cases for which the courtroom is best suited.

[19] *1964 Report of the Senate Judiciary Committee, op. cit.,* p. 36.

CHAPTER VI

INTERNATIONAL COMMERCIAL
ARBITRATION ·

THE DEVOTION OF AN ENTIRE CHAPTER to international commercial arbitration is, first and foremost, recognition of the fact that for most Western economies international commerce is expanding at a rate faster than domestic commerce. From 1950 to 1964, total world exports (F.O.B. in constant dollars) have increased from $57 billion to $151 billion, almost a threefold expansion.

Although U.S. exports have only risen from 15 billion in 1953 to 26 billion in 1964 (thus manifesting a decline by the U.S. exporting sector in its share of total world trade), our international community has more than made up for this relative decline by its energetic participation in investment abroad. Direct investment[1] abroad from 1958 to 1964 increased from $1,094 million to $2,297 million. What is labeled "other private long-term investment" in balance-of-payments terminology has increased during the same period from $1,444 million to $1,956 million.

The significant acceleration of activity by both U.S. international traders and investors has immediate relevance for our study of commercial arbitration. First, it is reasonable to assume that such vigorous expansion would give rise to an increasing number of disputes. While we are not suggesting a precisely linear relationship, evidence suggests that expansion of trade volume has a distinctly positive impact upon the incidence of disputes.

Second, the changing structure of our expanding international commerce must be noted. Investment constitutes an increasing share of our

---

[1] Direct investment implies a degree of management control and is generally limited to those cases in which at least 25 percent of the equity is held by a single U.S. resident or group of business-related residents. If some control is evident, however, equity ownership may be as low as 10 percent.

total commercial transactions with foreign countries. As a result, those institutions and procedures which, over the years, have evolved to deal with the problems of disputes in export-import trade may have to be re-examined in the light of the increasing importance of international investment and the unique problems which it poses.

Finally, the acceleration of international activity serves as an impressive and accentuating backdrop to the theme we shall be developing in this chapter. It is our contention that international commercial arbitration is, by and large, the most satisfactory vehicle for solving international disputes that have escalated beyond the party-to-party adjustment, negotiation, and accommodation stage. A significant corollary of this position is that commercial arbitration has more advantages as a dispute-settling vehicle in the international sphere than it has domestically. Implicit in this argument is a belief that international commercial arbitration is more than just a direct transfer of the arbitration mechanism to the international arena and more than domestic arbitration "writ large."

HISTORY

We will treat briefly those institutions, conventions, and customs that have historically given rise to the current state of international commercial arbitration. For our purposes it is useful to trace international commerce back to the era of the Crusades. It was at this time that the liberating influence of international trade possibilities was first felt by a medieval world deep in the clutches of economic provincialism and insularity:

> Strange though it may seem, medieval commerce developed from the beginning under the influence not of local but of export trade. It was this alone which gave birth to that class of professional merchants which was the chief instrument of the economic revival of the eleventh and twelfth centuries.[2]

Trade routes were expanded; where previously none existed, new routes were instituted. Without the aid of modern communications, these professional merchants had to meet face-to-face to carry on their activities. The bargaining for prices and the physical transfer of goods from one trader to another was an intensely personal affair. To accommodate the necessity for such personal encounters, trade transactions were geographi-

[2] H. Pirenne, *Economic and Social History of Medieval Europe* (New York: Harcourt, Brace and Company, 1937), p. 140.

cally institutionalized at fairs and certain port cities at various points throughout the Western World.

Because trade channels were still restricted and because of the necessity for significant personal contact, merchants began to develop and perceive a communal or collegial affiliation for one another. The constraints of geography—that is, the limited number of places where trade could take place—and the requirements for face-to-face transactions contributed to the identification of a merchant class.

It was not long before these merchants, recognizing a functional community among themselves, began instituting regulations pertaining to their trade activities. It is to these rudimentary medieval beginnings that legal historians trace the beginning of the "merchant's law" which was, to some degree, absorbed by the respective legal mechanisms of the nation states.

> The disputes of merchants at fairs in England were settled in the pie powder courts at which the actual decision was made by fellow merchants though the court might be nominally held by the lord of the fair or his bailiff. Further to be considered is the organization of English merchants who lived in towns into guild merchants. The guilds had adjudicatory machinery for disputes among members and this should perhaps be considered as being as much arbitration as the similar arrangements in exchanges and associations today.[3]

In the twelfth and thirteenth centuries, however, the forces of nationalism had yet to appear in full force. Instead, the Western World was chaotically subdivided into relatively autonomous fiefdoms, the product of the prevailing feudalistic social structure. The import of this social and political fact was that the forces and interests that bound together the merchants, plying their trade across fiefdom borders, were far more forceful bonds than were the customs and conventions prevailing among the scattered and decentralized political units. The merchant's law achieved a universality that stood in rather bold relief to the prevailing political and legal chaos.

It can be conjectured that the face-to-face contact at these fairs and port cities offered satisfactory communications and clear understanding of mutual intentions. Furthermore, the merchants were dealing with physical goods; the paperwork was minimal and not intricate. Both these factors would seem to indicate that the prospect of misunderstanding among merchants would be slight. However, history informs us that there

---

[3] W. C. Jones, "History of Commercial Arbitration in England and the United States: A Summary View," in M. Domke (ed.), *International Trade Arbitration* (New York: American Arbitration Association, 1958), p. 129.

was, indeed, the necessity for explicitly formulating rules and regulations and to provide for their observance.

The evolution of the merchant's law proceeded in a fashion not unlike common law, with the merchants themselves providing most of the input. It is interesting to note that legal norms regulating trade activity emanated in a pragmatic fashion from the merchant community itself. These tightly knit trade associations and guilds were also quite capable of judging and enforcing decisions among themselves.

In those times ostracism was a most effective enforcement weapon. The cohesive nature of these merchant groups permitted unified action that could result in a significant loss of privilege and opportunity for an obstinate trader. Trade channels were still narrow and restricted. A merchant could ill-afford to be on the "outs" with the controlling trade groups in one of the key commercial ports.

Even in those instances when the merchants needed recourse to the enforcement powers of the public authorities, they encountered little difficulty. In practically all trading communities, the customs and traditions embodied in the merchant's law were respected and upheld. In fact, in many of the port cities the merchant community dominated whatever form of government existed.

We have seen that, prior to the rigorous institution of nation states and their accompanying legal structures, the trading community had been able to regulate its own activities. The trading community, in contrast to the other elements in a chaotically decentralized society, had constructed what amounted to a legal fabric or mechanism around themselves. The arbitration mechanism is usually viewed as extra-legal. Yet, for the merchants, arbitration served as a law and legal system.

From an arbitral standpoint the important fact is, of course, that the traders were able to try and to resolve disputes among themselves. Just about the time, however, that merchants and traders were beginning to develop workable control mechanisms usable in most areas of the Western World, the phenomenon of nationalism began to emerge. The practical effect of this powerful force was the emasculation of the merchant's law as a universally applied doctrine. As the societies of these nation states became more settled, their legal systems became more developed. Admittedly, these judicial systems absorbed over a period of time the basic tenets of merchant contract and custom. The doctrine of legal sovereignty that surrounded the development of the judiciaries, however, severely curtailed international commercial proceedings and enforcement. As the legal structures of these nation states enveloped and cut across trading channels, it became increasingly difficult for internation commercial disputes to be settled in the courts of the respective countries.

The quasi-legal proceedings carried on within the trade and guild associations to resolve disputes were forced into the extra-legal sphere by the judicial system of the states.

The efforts of the international commercial community to circumvent the newly developing legal structure can be traced to two primary motivations. First, the historic rationale for industry or merchant adjudication was, of course, that those intimately familiar with the trade and its sometimes unwritten customs would be in the best position to judge commercial disputes. In many instances, the judgment proceedings could take place right at the trading site, thus providing fast and efficient justice. (This reasoning is similar to that described in those chapters dealing exclusively with domestic arbitration.)

Second, there was a less explicit recognition among the trading community that extra-legal arbitration could present itself as a subtle means of avoiding the legal sovereignty barriers that are posed by the recognition and enforcement of internation litigation.

The groping for an extra-legal dispute-settling mechanism took on added significance as the nature of international trade became more impersonal. As the volume of trade expanded, so did the number of trade channels. As the trading functions became more specialized, there was less of a need for face-to-face encounter. Commercial negotiations conducted at a distance had far greater potential for disputes. Furthermore, ostracism and self-policing among the trading groups no longer were powerful enforcement mechanisms.

Quite predictably, arbitration flourished in the ensuing centuries as an extra-legal mechanism in those countries which historically had been important centers for international trade and commerce. London, in particular, developed and nurtured various commodity and trade-oriented arbitration facilities:

> In the nineteenth century, the evidences of arbitration in England are quite plentiful. There were many textbooks written on the subject, and the Arbitration Act was amended in 1888 to provide for the enforcement of agreements to arbitrate future disputes. The most important development was, however, the wide-spread use of arbitrations in Trade Associations and Exchanges such as the Liverpool Cotton Exchange, the London Stock Exchange, the London Corn and Coffee Trade Association.[4]

Equally important, those countries with developed arbitration facilities

[4] *Ibid.,* p. 133.

also provided legal recognition of, and provisions for, the enforcement of arbitral contracts and awards. The problems associated with internation enforcement and recognition, in the case of England, were less crucial because much of the trade and disputes centered around London involved Commonwealth partners. The Commonwealth provided an effective umbrella under which the awards arising from international arbitration could be adequately enforced.

The Hanseatic trade centers of northern Germany were also active centers for international commercial arbitration. Here also trade practices and international preoccupations of medieval times spawned quite extensive and sophisticated trade arbitration facilities. However, in this case, the knotty problems of internation enforcement were more critical as there was no Commonwealth umbrella to provide the enforcing sanctions.

In the United States the first modern arbitration statute was enacted in New York in 1920. Significantly, New York was the state most actively engaged in international trade. In fact, a substantial number of those promoting the bill in the state legislature were leading importers, exporters, international bankers, and manufacturers.

Even though the primary international trading states of the Western World had enacted arbitration statutes by 1920, there was no provision in these national statutes guaranteeing the recognition of arbitral proceedings in foreign countries involving a national party. Just as the sovereignty motivations of the national legal systems hindered the enforcement of foreign legal judgments, the same national legalism interfered with the universal enforcement of arbitration provisions and awards. During the 1920's, therefore, significant efforts were made to secure among the important international trading nations common provisions for internation enforcement of arbitral awards.

Both the Geneva Protocol of 1923 and the companion Geneva Convention of 1927 dealt specifically with this problem. The United States, however, refused to participate in either. The United States' objections to the multilateral convention were based both on a constitutional reticence to enforce arbitration legislation through Congressional treaty power upon the states (at this time few states had arbitration statutes) and on a legal conservatism that was later to find its full fruition in the Connally Reservation in 1946.

For two decades the leading trading nation of the world refused to participate in any agreements, conventions, or treaties that would formally assure enforcement of foreign awards and contracts. During this time, however, the machinery and institutions engaged in international arbitration continued to make progress. In 1921 the newly formed International Chamber of Commerce (I.C.C.) established a centralized arbitration tribunal open to all traders. In 1934 the Inter-American Commercial Arbitration Commission was organized by the American Arbitration Association and the Council on Inter-American Relations.

These international arbitration tribunals filled an important void. Until this time, practically all of the international tribunals had been organized around the trade of a particular commodity or group of commodities. Availability of such general-purpose commissions vastly increased the spectrum of opportunities in which international arbitration could play an effective dispute-settling role.

There is a tendency among those who criticize and dramatize the failure to secure official multilateral recognition of foreign arbitration awards to forget that meaningful arbitral mechanisms must first be built upon well-established and respected tribunals. The development of both uniform and acceptable procedures and a sizable list of knowledgeable arbitrators from many different countries is a necessary step for any tribunal that is to command internation respect. These prerequisites were provided by such institutions as I.C.C. as their facilities grew and matured. By the end of World War II, I.C.C. had developed, through its main office in Paris, arbitration facilities that spanned a wide portion of the world. Equally important, I.C.C. had at its disposal a list of respected and competent arbitrators from different countries of the trading world.

From 1945 till the present time, the U.S. Government has given added impetus, albeit in a most restrained manner, to international arbitration by providing for a limited arbitration agreement in its Friendship, Commerce, and Navigation (F.C.N.) Treaties with foreign governments. The basic thrust of these agreements is that domestic courts would recognize foreign arbitral awards somewhat to the extent that they would be recognized if carried out within domestic jurisdiction. In effect, international arbitration can be pursued no more vigorously than the legal acceptance of its domestic counterpart will permit. Such bilateral treaties have been signed by the United States with 15 nations including France, West Germany, Italy, and Japan.

In recent years the United Nations has become actively involved in international arbitration. Under the auspices of the United Nations Economic and Social Council, the Economic Commission for Europe (E.C.E.) and Economic Commission for Asia and the Far East (ECAFE) have conducted rather exhaustive studies of the current state of arbitration procedures in their respective geographical areas.

Primarily as a result of such undertakings the Economic and Social Council sponsored a Convention on the Recognition and Enforcement of Foreign Arbitral Awards in May 1958. Embodying what many legal experts considered to be useful and more helpful clarifications of enforcement provisions contained in the Geneva Convention of 1927, this Convention once again attempted to come to grips with the age-old problems of legal sovereignty and multiplicity of arbitration statutes. As of May 1965, 29 nations have become signatories: among them are France, West Germany, Japan, India, Norway, and U.S.S.R. In most instances, the signing nations attached reciprocity provisos. As of May 1965 the United States had yet to sign. (The rather complex issue of U.S. and foreign recognition of international arbitral awards will be treated more extensively later in this chapter.)

In concluding this section on the history of international arbitration, we should note that a further and more complicating dimension has been added to the field of international transactions and its dispute settling mechanisms. The proliferation of capital and industrial property movements from this country abroad, in conjunction with the exuberant nationalism of the newly independent states of the underdeveloped world, has resulted in a vast array of investment disputes that transcend the export-import orientation of many contemporary arbitration tribunals. In recognition of this development, the International Bank for Reconstruction and Development (World Bank) submitted (March 18, 1965) to member governments a Convention on the Settlement of Investment Disputes between States and Nationals of Other States. It recommends the establishment of yet another extra-legal arbitral institution staffed by arbitrators picked by member governments. As such, it would utilize the time-honored arbitral mechanism, yet disassociate itself from the specifics of its commercial milieu.

Finally, we note that our survey of historical developments in the area of international commercial arbitration has revealed an interesting circular trend. In this country, arbitration received much of its initial impetus from the actions of the international trading and investment community. For the next several decades its primary focus was domestic in nature. Recent events, however, have once again brought to light the significant relevance commercial arbitration has for international disputes. It was, after all, among the international traders of antiquity that commercial arbitration was first conceived. In the following sections we will be exploring much more explicitly those unique features of both international trade per se and the commercial disputes which it engenders.

UNIQUE CHARACTERISTICS OF
INTERNATIONAL TRANSACTIONS

At the beginning of the chapter the point was made that international commercial arbitration was more than just domestic arbitration "writ large." In this section we should like to develop this theme by exploring some of the unique characteristics of international transactions with particular emphasis on their implications for the nature of dispute incidence and settlement.

PHYSICAL DISTANCES INVOLVED

Although there are, of course, exceptions to the following generalization, the distances spanned by international commerce are often greater than the distances spanned by its domestic counterpart. Mundane as this generalization appears, it nevertheless has important implications for the nature of international dispute incidence and settlement.

Frequently, the distances that separate the parties of a given international commercial transaction require communication by mail rather than by telephone or by face-to-face encounter. Such long-distance negotiations are bound to have an impact upon the degree of understanding that can be embodied within a given contractual arrangement. Whether the contract in question covers the shipment of goods or the assignment of a patent, successful and workable agreements require that each party understand the motivations and interests of the other as fully as possible. Distances can very easily inhibit the establishment of such necessary mutual understandings.

In the case of export-import trade, goods are generally involved in a longer transit with a greater opportunity for damage in transit. Even if the intentions of the traders are perfectly clear to one another, the methods of transport and the length of transit present opportunities for damage and delay that will require adjustment of some sort.

Once a dispute has occurred, the distances separating the parties to the contract hinder efforts in resolving the disputes. Depending on the nature of the dispute-settling mechanism, the transport of evidence—both animate and inanimate—to the site of adjudication can present difficulties.

We can see, therefore, that the complicating characteristics of geography and distance weave themselves, much as a contentious thread, throughout the dynamics of the international commercial process: contract provision, commodity transferal, and dispute resolution.

BARRIERS OF LANGUAGE AND COMMERCIAL CUSTOM

The impact of different languages and customs upon international commerce, as distinct from domestic commerce, is readily apparent. The problems posed by indigenous commercial customs are not as serious in European trade as they are in trade with many of the underdeveloped nations. The ethic of industrialization, with all its implications for commercial customs, has been with the Western World for several centuries. Such is decidedly not the case, however, with vast areas of Latin America, Africa, and Asia.

Furthermore, this problem has been accentuated in recent years by the rapid breakup of the vast colonial empires that extended over much of the underdeveloped world. In many instances the powerful forces of nationalism drastically altered the faces of those with whom the U.S. businessman had to deal at the other end of his contract. As Europeans were replaced with nationals, the uniformity of commercial customs that existed for the most part between Europeans and Americans was impaired.

DIFFERENCES IN COMMERCIAL LAW AMONG NATIONAL LEGAL SYSTEMS

Lawyers and businessmen alike agree that the difference within our own country among the commercial statutes of the respective states provides a disconcerting irritant to the problems of commercial contracting. If this lack of conformity is an irritant at the domestic level, it certainly is a significant barrier at the international level.

Domestically, the differences at least emanate from a basic common law background. Internationally, the differences are frequently magnified by an entirely different legal philosophy. The fundamental differences that exist between common law, Roman, and Asiatic legal backgrounds can, in some instances, be quite severe.

The full force of this complication is felt when a dispute over a given contract concerns a matter of law rather than fact. In this situation, the question of where adjudication of the dispute is sought is extremely important, and the construction of any commercial contract must of necessity be concerned with this problem. As we shall see later, when the parties are considering arbitration versus litigation, the factor of which country and which set of commercial statutes are to be invoked becomes extremely important.

The lengthy and complicated question of the impact that differing national legal systems have upon enforceability of contractual dispute judgments will be deferred to a later section. Suffice it to say, however, that different countries have entirely different attitudes concerning enforcement of judgments resulting from proceedings in a foreign country.

Differences in commercial law between legal systems, therefore, not only complicate the task of providing for adequate contracts in so far as differences in substantive law must be taken into account but also endanger enforceability of judgments that must cross national boundaries.

STATE INTERVENTION

Historically, it is true that governments have considered all commerce that involves domestic nationals and foreign nationals to be very much within their purview. Regardless of the laissez-faire attitude that may prevail with respect to domestic commerce, foreign commerce qualitatively constitutes a different type of transaction in terms of public interest.

This attitude of world governments has quite severe implications for those businessmen engaged in international commerce. For the U.S. businessman, headquartered in a country where governmental interference with domestic commerce is the exception rather than the rule, the transition to thinking in terms of possible impingement by public authorities can be difficult. He certainly is not conditioned to anticipate the many diverse facets of possible governmental interference.

Regardless of the rapport and understanding which a U.S. businessman may have achieved with a foreign party, the octopus-like tentacles of public control and regulation can appear at unpredictable times and with blinding speed, thus wreaking havoc with previous commercial arrangements. The variations on this rather invidious theme of governmental interference are, of course, many. The most immediately apparent category is the extensive set of weapons that any virile government has filed away in its trade restriction armory. Included among these are tariffs and quantitative quotas.

A more sophisticated set of controls that impinge not only on trade but also on capital movements resides in the government's ability to institute currency control and alter official exchange rates. Happily, the former restriction is rapidly disappearing in this age of trade liberalization. However, the potential for currency exchange-rate alteration will always remain to plague and render more unpredictable the commercial efforts of businessmen engaged in international commerce.

Another form of state obstructionism in the affairs of international commerce is the harassment of foreign-owned assets and the profits generated by them. This form of intervention has received considerable publicity in recent years as the various governments of the world, particularly in underdeveloped nations, have increasingly resorted to it.

This intervention can take several forms, with expropriation being, of course, the most dramatic. With regard to expropriation, there seems to be no practical alternative to admitting that governments do, in fact, have the right to invoke the doctrine of "public interest"—regardless of how ambiguously it is defined—and to seize assets under foreign ownership. The area where there does seem to be a possible use for arbitration is the nature and amount of reimbursement.

More subtle forms of state intervention involve the issues of profit distribution—to whom and how much—taxation, ownership, and employment restrictions.

All of these are areas in which foreign governments may unexpectedly appear and alter or actually invalidate the arrangements that private investors have previously made. Dispute potential is obviously significant. And yet it may frequently be impossible to make provisions and hedges against governmental interference by anticipation within the contract provisions. All the goodwill in the world between a U.S. corporation and a licensed distributor abroad will be to no avail if the foreign party to the transaction is nationalized. In such an instance, anticipatory protection for such intervention and subsequent disputes would require more than the assent of the foreign national. As we shall see later, new machinery and arrangements are being developed by foreign investors to deal with such dispute possibilities.

The important point that we want to convey is that the prospects for governmental intervention are far more likely among international transactions than they are among domestic transactions. Such likelihood breeds uncertainty; where there is such uncertainty, the potential for disputes is rife. There is, in addition, the significant point that the nature of the threat oftentimes precludes sufficient anticipatory protection within the provisions of the contract. Both of these factors should induce the U.S. businessman engaged in international commerce to reflect more closely than his domestic counterpart upon the initial incorporation of dispute-settling mechanisms in his contracts.

POLITICAL RECONSTITUTION OF MANY AREAS OF THE WORLD

As has been mentioned, the remarkable proliferation in recent years of newly independent nation states has provided a significant catalyst for the development of international commercial disputes. Previously where the U.S. businessman dealt with the colonial empires of Western Europe, he now deals with the many sovereignties into which the European holdings have been subdivided.

This subdivision has resulted in a proliferation of sovereign legal systems in areas formally encompassed by the vast uniformity of either Commonwealth or French law or whatever. While it is true that to a significant extent these new nations have carried on the legal traditions of their respective colonial systems, they have instituted their own variations and nuances.

Such a multiplicity quite clearly has contributed to the problems presented by differing commercial law statutes and enforcement procedures that have been alluded to earlier. Of equal importance, however, is the fact that accompanying this political reconstitution there has been a rather drastic restructuring of social and economic attitudes among the governing elite of these countries.

Among many of the officials, both political and economic, of these newly constituted nations there is a profound and deep-rooted suspicion of Western traditions, institutions, and its primary economic system of private enterprise. Such sentiments provide a most fertile milieu for the various types of governmental harassment and obstructions discussed earlier. It should be noted that this anti-Western sentiment frequently extends also to the arbitration tribunals which have evolved over the years. Such suspicion extends, therefore, from businessmen who do the trading and investing to the mechanisms they have developed to settle their disputes.

Not unexpectedly, the political and economic attitudes of these new nations have been translated into a socialistic orientation for their domestic economies. Increasingly, U.S. businessmen have had to deal with foreign governments in their capacity as managers of production. Frequently, in having to deal with a government directly as the other party to a contractual agreement, the range of methods for resolving disputes is limited. In many countries the government and its agencies are explicitly forbidden to have disputes arbitrated; the disputes must be adjudicated in the courts.

THE HISTORICALLY DOMESTIC ORIENTATION OF U.S. BUSINESSMEN

The recent acceleration of foreign commercial commitments and oftentimes the related unfamiliar contracts have tended to highlight and emphasize the relative unfamiliarity of a vast segment of American businessmen with the intricacies of international transactions.

Historically, this country has been economically self-sufficient. As recently as 1962, gross exports and imports of goods and services constituted only 5.6 percent and 5.5 percent, respectively, of total gross national product. The corresponding figures in both Britain and West Germany are upwards of 20 percent.

Contracts negotiated between parties in New York and Calcutta, for example, have significantly greater uncertainties and variables than do similar undertakings between New York and Chicago, as we have pointed out in previous paragraphs. Whereas the English businessman has been confronting these types of problems for centuries, his American counterpart is a relative novice.

This rather general and impressionistic observation serves as a useful concluding comment in this section wherein we have attempted to portray the differentiating characteristics of international commerce, with particular emphasis on their implications for the nature of dispute incidence and settlement.

Our position is that the international area presents problems and difficulties that make preparation for dispute contingencies more imperative and requisite for the international businessman than for the domestically oriented businessman. In following sections we shall explore more systematically the specific nature of these transaction categories and the respective organizational entities that undertake them.

TYPES OF INTERNATIONAL TRANSACTIONS WITH UNIQUE DISPUTE CHARACTERISTICS

We shall endeavor to categorize international commercial transactions by type. Such a segmentation can be useful in isolating those elements of a given transaction that make certain types of dispute adjudications appropriate.

EXPORT-IMPORT TRADE

Historically, it has been the import-export trade to which international commercial arbitration has been most frequently applied. The reasons for this are not difficult to find. The disputes that emanate from a contract for a shipment of goods are of a rather predictable variety, all of which are susceptible to the advantages which arbitration has to offer.

First and foremost, these disputes are concerned mainly with facts rather than law, and these facts are generally of a quantifiable and, therefore, determinable nature. Essential contract provisions most frequently involve factors such as number, weight, volume, delivery date, and quality. With the exception of quality, these factors are all precisely determinable. Even the question of quality is a reasonably calculable attribute in the hands of a skilled and practiced industry authority. The potential for disputes is usually centered about the goods themselves.

As a result of this product orientation, anticipatory dispute protection can be precise and neatly provided for. There need be no vague and general arbitral clause that legitimizes an unknown spectrum of disputes. Rather, the clause can be specific and clearly define those issues which are to be arbitrated.

An executive for the international division of a well-known food processor states: "Normally, in a business like ours there would be two basic reasons for the eventual or possible necessity of arbitration; one would be failure to perform as per contract on such matters as deliveries and the other would be the question of grade or quality." These, then, are the types of disputes that arise out of export and import trade transactions.

As the following extract from the purchase-sale form for the company indicates, the jurisdiction of the arbitration is precisely delineated: "Disputes concerning short delivery or non-delivery or late delivery shall be submitted to arbitration in San Francisco and shall be conducted in accordance with rules of the Canners League of California." The contract provision also brings out another relevant point. In most instances the nature of export-import transactions are centralized around key ports of entry and deal with commodities that are bought and sold by many people. This type of situation is suitable for the development of industry associations that can provide the encouragement and expertise in arranging internal adjudication.

In the opinion of the authors, these types of transactions lend themselves most favorably to those attributes and advantages of arbitration that have been developed in previous chapters.

LICENSING

In this category we mean to include all possible variations in the international transfer of industrial property and industrial know-how by a licensing contract. In addition to the terms of transfer, the license also includes specific royalty or remunerative provisions.

A licensing agreement is a far more complex document than the purchase-and-sale agreement associated with export-import trade. There are many more provisions. Satisfactory performance of the transfer by the licensee in most instances requires observance of a significant number of proscriptions set up by the licensor. On the other hand, the licensee is motivated to specify the type of activity to which he is entitled with the acquiring of this industrial property or know-how.

As a result of the motivation to specify as precisely as possible all the rights and restrictions the licensee must observe, this type of contract of necessity will be lengthy and complex. Its construction alone will require more legal technicalities than would a trade document. Another facet of this type of contract in the international sphere is that the substantive issue of appropriate law in the respective countries is crucial. The nature of the transaction, more so than with export-import agreements, brings the contracting provisions into the domain of the legal statutes of the respective countries.

We said earlier that with purchase-sale–agreements disputes arose primarily from questions of fact rather than law. With licensing contracts, however, the dispute is much more likely to be of a legal nature. This differentiating characteristic, of course, has implications for the type of dispute-settling mechanism that is resorted to by the parties.

A further point to be made is that even the nature of the factual dispute, when it occurs, poses more difficulties. We mentioned that with purchase-sale contracts the facts relevant to the provision in question are easily determinable. With licensing this is not necessarily the case. Purchase-sale agreements are tied to the satisfactory supply of a good or service. Conveying limited title to a patent, trademark, or some sort of industrial know-how is a far more intangible type of transaction. The nature of an export-import transaction brings both buyer and seller physically to grips with the question of whether their respective performances met specifications. Feedback as to contract violation of a license is indirect and uncertain. The nature of the transaction, per se, does not bring contract violation to light. In most instances such evidence must be autonomously generated by one of the parties.

A further complicating feature of a licensing contract revolves around contract clause interpretation. Not only are the relevant facts sometimes difficult to seek out but also there can be disputes over what type of performance a given provision specifies. Both of these characteristics require a more formalized and detached deliberative institution for dispute settling. These disputes are not matters determinable on the docks and wharves of the ports of entry as purchase-sale contracts frequently are. Evidence must be carefully sifted and procured, and the implications of contract provisions must be rigorously scrutinized and analyzed by a perceptive mind.

If arbitration is to be employed as the dispute-settling medium in international licensing agreements, it will have to possess some unique features. Arbitration associated with export-import trade is most frequently carried on by institutions internal to the specific industry groups. This is natural because the economic activity associated with purchase-sale contracts usually clusters around an industry grouping and facilitates scrutiny by appropriate trade associations. Also, knowledge of industry customs and traditions is necessary in order to evaluate such matters as quality performance.

Licensing arrangements, however, infrequently cluster in such a way as to encourage industry control. They are more isolated and independent contracts. Adjudication of these types of disputes requires less industry knowledge and more general capabilities in commercial contract interpretation. If international litigation were not such a complex and difficult procedure, it would probably be a forum for such disputes. However, in recognition of these complexities, we consider that general arbitration tribunals, such as the American Arbitration Association and I.C.C., provide more feasible mechanisms.

INVESTMENT ABROAD

The statistics quoted at the beginning of this chapter revealed the dramatically increasing extent to which the American businessman is investing abroad. Earlier we discussed some of the special problems that a foreign investor might encounter, mostly in the form of governmental harassment.

The unique aspect of the foreign investment transaction lies in the fact that there does not necessarily have to be a contractual partner. In the case of both export-import trade and industrial property transfer, we saw that a contractual arrangement was an integral part of the transaction. These contracts quite clearly provide a convenient vehicle on which to append dispute-settling provisions. If, however, an American corporation is constructing a plant abroad, there are no contractual arrangements that arise from its act of investing, per se.

A realization of this brings one squarely to grips with the critical fact that the potential for dispute arises not from the commercial community and its frailties but from the rather ominous quarter of public intervention. If the businessman desires some measure of protection for his foreign assets and operations, he must rely upon either the local judiciary, U.S. Government support, or an autonomously sought out arbitral agreement with the public authority of the country involved. The salient fact is that anticipatory dispute protection must be autonomously sought out by the investing party. A separate contract, exclusively concerned with dispute settling, must be drawn up. As we have seen in other international transactions, this type of provision can usually be appended to the contract that accompanies the transaction—whether it be a purchase-sale or licensing agreement. (The advantages of the above-mentioned methods of dispute settling will be dealt with in a following section.)

The one type of investment abroad wherein a second commercial party might be involved in the act of investment, per se, is the rather recently developed organizational entity, the joint venture. In this situation the American firm shares the equity ownership of the assets with a group of foreign nationals. Such an arrangement is usually prompted by the actions of the foreign government in its attempt to avoid the possibility of absentee ownership.

It is frequently in the interest of the parties to the joint venture to arrange for a contract covering their respective rights and duties in the operational control of the assets in question. This is a relatively new form of contractual provision. Yet we anticipate its increased utilization as the type of transaction that fostered it, the joint venture, seems likely to receive renewed emphasis in this age of sensitive nationalism. As is readily apparent, this type of contractual arrangement once again provides the businessman with a convenient vehicle for an arbitral dispute-settling provision. A major U.S. corporation indicated:

> At present this corporation has several foreign joint ventures, each partner having 50% control. Although the instance has yet to occur of the deadlock of the Board of Directors, the arbitration provision in these joint venture agreements will hopefully provide a speedy solution should difficulties arise. I mention this use of arbitration as it may be a bit novel.

More than any other type of transaction, foreign investment illustrates the unique problems that beset the businessman engaged in international commerce. There certainly is no domestic counterpart to the real concern which an international investor must evidence toward the actions of the public authorities.

INTERNATIONAL DISPUTE-SETTLING MECHANISMS

In this section, we shall discuss the dispute-settling mechanisms that are available for those involved in international transactions. With regard to international commercial arbitration, we will once again dwell upon only those aspects of the process which have not been touched upon in the preceding chapters.

Throughout our discussion of dispute-settling mechanisms, we will introduce the results of a questionnaire sent to over 100 top executives engaged in international commerce. Over 50 percent of this group responded, representing a wide cross section of manufacturers, distributors, and bankers. By including these results, we will endeavor to relate current attitudes and practices in the business community to the hypotheses that have evolved from our discussion of international commerce.

FACE-TO-FACE NEGOTIATION AND ADJUSTMENT

Both international and domestic businessmen go to considerable length to avoid the use of any third-party mechanism or other outside system to settle their commercial disputes. Motivations for the avoidance of this formal recourse are, of course, many. We believe the following quotes accurately represent the attitudes of the international business community regarding the importance of face-to-face negotiation and adjustment.

> We currently purchase merchandise from 21 different countries. Our imports cover finished consumer goods, component parts, and raw materials. We set up contracts with the foreign sources on all purchases. These contracts do not include an arbitration clause. It has been our feeling that *direct contact* with the sources in adjusting problems and claims is more satisfactory and we have not wanted to open the door to international commercial arbitration. To date we have found that where problems have arisen that the sources have been willing and anxious to work out a mutually satisfactory settlement with us. [Emphasis ours.]

> In most instances we buy from sources on a continuing basis and thereby develop a good business relationship the same as we do in the United States. We are fully aware of the possibilities of commercial arbitration and would suggest such means of settlement were we to find, in a particular instance, that direct settlement cannot be made. We prefer, however, to hold such action as a final means of settlement rather than make it a normal part of procedure.

This particular company, therefore, places the same emphasis domestically and internationally on the avoidance of any third-party mechanism. Interestingly enough, however, it did indicate that if personal negotiations were to fail, it would suggest international commercial arbitration as a means of settlement. The use of the phrase "continuing basis" is consistent with the overall response from our international questionnaire. Over 50 percent of the respondents specifically mentioned that continuing relationships were more important internationally than domestically. Such a belief would seem to indicate an even greater desire to avoid and prevent disputes among international businessmen. Derivatively, we would expect that where avoidance of a formal dispute was impossible, international businessmen would be motivated to utilize the most expedient and informal dispute-settling mechanism possible.

Even those businessmen who regularly utilize arbitration clauses in their international contracts recognize that the real solution is to resolve the disputes among themselves: "Whereas I would certainly recommend incorporating a clause calling for arbitration, even arbitration is expensive and time consuming, and it is usually very advisable for every effort to be made to resolve disputes without having to fall back on this device."

It is unfortunate that in a situation where continuing relationships assume such significance, the problems of distance and communication (as developed previously) often preclude the frequent interaction which fosters amiable, dispute-free relationships. It could very well be that international businessmen place a significant value on continuing relationships precisely because the environment presents such wide potential for disputes. The international businessman must realistically recognize that face-to-face negotiation will frequently be impossible.

NATIONAL JUDICIARIES

The problems and inconveniences associated with court adjudication of domestic commercial disputes have been well documented in previous chapters. In this section, we will highlight those features that, by and large, make the courts even less suitable as dispute-settling mechanisms in the international area.

Of immediate and prime importance is the sheer multiplicity of laws and statutes that must be considered. Modern communication and transportation facilities have enabled the businessman to construct amazingly complex trade apparatuses that are, typically, based in some three or four countries. While the businessman may have been liberated from geographical constraints, he still has to contend with the legal sovereignties of the countries involved, however. The following quotation illustrates this situation most aptly:

> On the Continent of Europe there are in effect more laws than there are states. . . . In a flight of less than three hours a traveller may cross above territories with four or five different legal systems. Two businessmen from A and B meeting at an aerodrome of country C and concluding there an agreement for a contract relating some staple commodity produced in country D c.i.f. a port in country E, against documents to be presented to a bank in country F—this is not an imaginary case. [One] may have to enlist the services of six experts on the six different legal systems that may be involved.[5]

Businessmen quite naturally shudder at the prospect of confronting such a maze of "red tape." The same type of difficulties involved in the drawing of a contract will be manifested in attempts to settle disputes arising from such contracts in the courts. A good contract can frequently specify the country whose courts will be used to settle disputes. This does not circumvent the problem entirely, however.

Local counsel will undoubtedly have to be obtained to provide the necessary familiarity with the intricacies of the law in the country involved. The rather intricate and involved rules of evidence will frequently require inconvenient travel and valuable time in order to assemble the required testimony and documents.

The American Bar Association stated that with "the expansion of international trade in recent years, the business world has been increasingly reluctant to litigate in foreign courts of law differences arising from international commercial transactions."[6] A senior legal officer on the staff of the United Nations says:

> When, however, it becomes necessary to resort to the machinery of justice to settle a dispute connected with the contract (international commercial transaction), the jet gives way to the horse-and-buggy. To obtain and enforce a judgment in another country is still a complicated, time-consuming, and expensive operation.[7]

In view of the increasing importance of American investment abroad,

---

[5] E. J. Cohn, "Economic Integration and International Commercial Arbitration," in M. Domke (ed.), *International Trade Arbitration* (New York: American Arbitration Association, 1958), p. 19.

[6] C. J. Hynning, *et al., Report of the Committee on International Unification of Private Law* (Washington, D.C.: American Bar Association, May 1960), p. 4.

[7] Contini, "International Commercial Arbitration: United Nations Convention on the Recognition and Enforcement of Foreign Arbitral Awards," 8 *American Journal of Comp. Law.* 283 (1959).

there is another facet to the inconveniences associated with court settlements. Many respected commentators in the field of international law seem to feel that there is some doubt as to the fairness of a judgment rendered by a foreign court where the defendant, the government of the country, has been accused of illegal intervention with the assets of a non-national:

> The American investor, dissatisfied with an investment situation in a foreign country, will not be inclined to go before the courts of that country. He will be fearful of the nationalistic trend in those courts, especially when a vital question of the country's interest is involved. Rightly or wrongly the mere suspicion is enough to make one look for other means of relief.[8]

The American Bar Association refers to "the hostility of many parts of the world to legal or contractual measures for the protection of the private rights of foreign individuals and entities."[9]

The import of these politely phrased quotations is that the American investor abroad should, indeed, be suspicious of the nature of the legal judgments he is likely to receive in foreign courts. Yet it is primarily in those countries where the businessman can expect governmental harassment that he has most reason to be suspicious of the nationalism permeating the judiciary.

One company responding to our questionnaire has proceeded from these same facts and reached a contradictory conclusion. Because of the nature of this company's business, it is completely dependent upon a highly flexible yet adequate labor supply. Such dependency has led it to a policy of complete commitment to the differing environments of a number of countries. The company indicated that

> . . . operations require that we enter a host country under a set of circumstances wherein permanency in such a host country is a principal consideration. In effect, we have to think in terms of living in the host country and, generally, for an indefinitely extended period of time and even permanently. Under these circumstances we must expect to submit to, and rely upon, the same institutions as those available to and used by the nationals, in most cases. Among these institutions, of course, are the local legal, judicial and court systems.

[8] M. Domke, "The Settlement of International Investment Disputes," *The Business Lawyer,* Vol. 12 (April 1957), p. 265. It was stated in a report of the Netherlands Branch of the International Law Association that "the indispensable objectivity and impartiality are sometimes jeopardized by considerations of national interest; this occurs especially in cases in which considerable interests are at stake." Report of the Fortieth Conference, International Law Association, 174 (Amsterdam, 1938).

[9] C. J. Hynning, *et al., op. cit.,* p. 2.

Realizing that absentee ownership is a sensitive issue, the company concluded that the best way to exist in this environment was to indicate a willingness to be governed by the "laws of the land." Thus, when disputes arose, they were submitted to the local courts for settlement. This company noted that: "it has generally been our policy and practice to rely upon the local court system in any cases where enforcement of contract terms might extend themselves to such a point." In contrast, however, a company with lesser commitment in a foreign country and less dependence upon national goodwill would most likely question the wisdom of submitting a dispute to the foreign judiciary.

In addition to this example, 50 percent of the manufacturers responding to our questionnaire favored litigation over arbitration. The attitude of each manufacturer was most likely a reflection of the firm's legal counsel. Reasons given for favoring litigation included:

- Past experience.
- Legal fraternity objects to commercial arbitration.
- Legal rights better protected, but depends on the country.
- Firm rules.
- No further recourse in commercial arbitration.
- Reliability of accepted procedure.

The reasons given by international businessmen who favor litigation are similar to those offered by their domestic counterparts. In international commerce, litigation offers no additional advantages beyond those developed in earlier chapters dealing with the domestic businessman. Actually, there are two significant characteristics that make its use even more difficult than in domestic markets. First and foremost are the problems and difficulties associated with working through the differing laws of the various national legal systems. Second, there seems to exist considerable doubt about the impartiality of foreign judiciaries in disputes involving their government and an outside investor.

INTERNATIONAL LEGAL BODIES

Through the centuries, statesmen have sought to institute a supranational mechanism that would enable the world's nations and their citizens to resolve their disputes amicably under the rule of law. Frustrating these efforts has been a cruel yet unremitting paradox that thwarts today's internationalists. Nations will not relinquish their legal sovereignty for the very reason that brought about the dispute and hostility to begin with: countries of the world do not perceive their respective self-interests to be compatible over a sufficiently broad range of human activity. In this country, the Connally Reservation reflected the extent to which the U.S. Congress felt there was a commonality of interest among the nations of the world.

It is for reasons such as these that today's International Court of Justice (I.C.J.), the legal arm of the United Nations, has had such little effect on the affairs of the world. The area wherein the Court has compulsory jurisdiction is narrow. A further problem arises from the fact that the Court will consider disputes only between governments. The effect of this limitation is that, for all practical purposes, the businessman has no recourse to such tribunals for prosecution of a claim against a foreign government.

In theory, it may be possible for the businessman to press his claim against a foreign government through the public authorities of his own country. Evidence suggests, however, that very rarely will a government take on a case for one of its citizens and press charges at the International Court against the foreign government in question: "While States are sometimes willing to bring before the Court claims based on injuries to individuals or corporations many private claimants have found that the Foreign Offices of their countries are usually very reluctant to press claims against other governments."[10] It has been alleged, for instance, that Foreign Offices have two standard answers to requests of private claimants: (1) "our relations with the other State are so bad we don't want to pour additional oil on the fire," or (2) "our relations with the other State are so good that we don't want to spoil them by arguing about petty claims."

Only in the situation where the businessman is involved in a dispute with a foreign government would it be possible for I.C.J. to provide judgment. As we have seen, even in this instance the chances are slim either that the government will plead the case or that the foreign government will recognize the Court's jurisdiction. In any event, I.C.J. does not provide the businessman engaged in international commerce with a very usable facility for settling disputes.

It seems that there exists a rather remarkable parallel between the legitimacy of the international legal system that has evolved over the years and present day international arbitration facilities. Neither of the institutions looks to a higher form of a supranational political body from which to derive its authority and legitimacy. Rather, both mechanisms derive

---

[10] L. B. Sohn, "Proposals for the Establishment of a System of International Tribunals," in M. Domke (ed.), *International Trade Arbitration* (New York: American Arbitration Association, 1958), p. 65.

whatever sustenance and strength they possess from the respective nation states of the world.

It would seem that the forces and community of interest that pervade a nation state impart to the domestic judiciary a certain legitimacy and finality. Domestically, therefore, commercial arbitration must clearly derive its sanction from the legal statutes of the land. The attitude of the domestic courts is a permissive one: *allowing* individuals to contract initially out of the courts' domain but then reappearing as the enforcement agency.

There is no such relationship between the international courts and arbitration. Both these institutions derive their legitimacy from the respective nation states that see fit to delegate some degree of jurisdiction to them. Clearly, the international arbitration tribunals do not receive their sanction from the International Court of Justice.

In this regard, it is interesting to note that historically the idea for a permanent international court emanated from the prevailing arbitration practices of the world's governments. In 1899 Elihu Root, U.S. Secretary of State, in instructions to the U.S. delegation to the Second Hague Conference, observed that the principal objection to arbitration rested not upon the unwillingness of nations to submit their controversies to impartial arbitration but upon an apprehension that the arbitrators would not be impartial. He instructed the delegates to have the Permanent Court of Arbitration developed into a permanent tribunal composed of judges "who are judicial officers and nothing else, who are paid adequate salaries, who have no other occupation and who will devote their entire time to the trial and decision of inter-nation causes by judicial methods and under a sense of judicial responsibility."[11]

Since these two mechanisms are conceptually similar, it is interesting to speculate why international adjudication as a dispute-settling mechanism has prospered while the International Court has remained relatively inactive. The most obvious explanation has to do with the fact that the two institutions are dealing with significantly different types of disputes. Public disputes between nation states can hardly be compared with the commercial disagreements that face the arbitration tribunals.

It seems that the nation states have been far more willing, either explicitly or implicitly, to relinquish their legal sovereignty in commercial matters than in questions that involve broad social and political interests. (Interestingly, this question of public interest has finally found its way

[11] *Encyclopaedia Britannica*, Vol. 12 (1964), p. 513.

into international arbitration as well. As we have discussed previously, the businessman is increasingly involved in disputes with governments as they participate and intervene within their respective economies. Only time will tell to what extent these governments will be willing to treat their own activity either as "commercial" and therefore establishing at least an adjudicable dialogue with the individual or as "public" and therefore nontransferable to the realm of international arbitration.) As we shall see later, this relinquishment, curiously enough, has been manifested more in the recognition of international arbitration awards than in the recognition of judgments of other national judiciaries.

INTERNATIONAL COMMERCIAL ARBITRATION FACILITIES

It is frequently helpful when talking about arbitration facilities to separate them by the degree of their formalization. Following this framework, we shall first take up those arbitration mechanisms that over the years have become institutionalized.

Trade tribunals. As we have seen in the section on history and in the section on trade transactions, industry arbitration facilities have played an important role in the history of international arbitration. There are countless hundreds of these facilities organized by industries and by port cities throughout the world. There is no question that they provide a useful and necessary service for their members. Their worth is probably even more significant in the international area because of the hardship imposed by the distances and the complexities of the national legal systems. Among those industries that are sufficiently homogeneous to make arbitration facilities workable, circumvention of the national courts constitutes a significant plus for all the familiar reasons: time, expense, expertise, and so on.

As one would expect, these industry tribunals are concerned almost exclusively with the export and import trade of the industry commodity. Occasionally, it happens that traders in other goods will bring disputes before them, inasmuch as the particular tribunal may have an outstanding reputation for expertise and speed. Such infrequent occurrences, however, should not obscure the fact that these industry arbitration facilities are very much specialized.

Historically, these industry-oriented tribunals have their antecedents in the various guild and merchant groupings discussed earlier. It is interesting to note that not all of the vitality of their internal policing powers has been vitiated over the centuries. To this extent their arbitration activities enjoy a certain immunity from the contemporary difficulties associated with internation award enforcement. Their internal regulatory powers still have considerable bite; withdrawal of association privileges is frequently a threat sufficient to enforce compliance with tribunal awards.

In fact, it is this very internal power of the industry that has prompted some considerable criticism. One group of critics contends that such untrammeled private power constitutes a threat to the liberties of the individual traders in the industry. A private, unregulated cartelization of commercial power is the fear of such groups. Yet the realities of actual practice seem to indicate that such "private power" has provided a useful service both to the industry, in minimizing the time and expense involved in commercial disputes, and to the public, by freeing valuable court time from such specialized disputes.

Regional tribunals. The next step up from the very specialized facilities are those arbitration tribunals that define their area of competence not by industrial commodities but by geographic region. Two notable examples of this are the American Arbitration Association and the Inter-American Commercial Arbitration Commission.

These tribunals are not oriented around the trade of a particular industry. They are called upon to settle both trade disputes involving a broad spectrum of commodities and contract disputes involving licensing agreements and other more exotic contractual forms pertaining to international commerce. We noted in previous sections that adjudication of disputes arising from licensing contracts may require different arbitral skills than adjudication of those arising from purchase-sale contracts. Specifically, the arbitrator must rely more upon basic intellectual competence in interpreting the contract provisions and in sifting through the relevant facts than upon acquired industry expertise. In our opinion, this requirement demands from the arbitrators a competence considerably beyond simple business or industry familiarity.

The matter of staffing these general purpose tribunals with competent arbitrators is a difficult undertaking. This is particularly true in the international area where it is important to secure the services of arbitrators from several different countries. Oftentimes, these geographical prerequisites can not be aligned with the supply of acceptable talent. One international firm polled by the authors was, in fact, most unhappy with arbitrator competence: "In the past, our company has had considerable experience with arbitration abroad. Our experience has been largely unhappy because of the low caliber of the arbitrators who have been assigned to cases in which we were a party." We do not mean to indict, by this isolated instance, the qualifications of the arbitrators employed by these international tribunals. We believe, however, that this does point out a hazard that should be recognized and dealt with explicitly. Despite its experience, the firm continues to recognize the advantages offered by commercial arbitration in international commerce. It went on to note that arbitration "in international commerce has great possibility and I do not believe our experience necessarily indicates any basic inadequacy of the arbitration concept. It is simply that we have developed a very cautious attitude because of our past experience."

International Chamber of Commerce (I.C.C.). A third privately institutionalized tribunal is the International Chamber of Commerce Court of Arbitration. This tribunal accepts disputes emanating from practically any type of commercial contract originating in any part of the world. In the *News Bulletin* for the Economic Committee for Asia and the Far East, I.C.C. has provided some interesting statistics on the nature of disputes it has arbitrated and the place of origin of those disputes.[12]

Since I.C.C.'s inception in 1921, over 5,000 parties have been involved in the 2,000 disputes submitted to it. Recently, there has been an average of 50 disputes per year submitted. In commenting on this seemingly small number of disputes, I.C.C. stated:

> However, it must be remembered that the cases submitted to the I.C.C. are of a special nature. Whereas arbitration organized within the trades is generally confronted only with difficulties concerning the quality of a product, which is dealt with by procedure akin to a valuation, I.C.C. arbitration concerns itself with cases more complex and, fortunately, more rare than disputes concerning the quality of goods.

> 22 European countries have produced 253 plaintiffs and 246 defendants.

> The American continent has produced 26 plaintiffs and 33 defendants.

> The participation of Asia and Africa is identical, being 18 plaintiffs and 13 defendants on the one hand, and 15 plaintiffs and 12 defendants on the other.

> Europe has supplied 146 arbitrators; America, 6 arbitrators; and Asia and Africa, 2 arbitrators.

> The nature of the disputes submitted to the I.C.C. arbitration makes any attempt at classification according to trades and industries or by classes of goods extremely difficult. Only a classification based on the subject,

---

[12] Economic Commission for Asia and the Far East, "ECAFE Center for the Promotion of Commercial Arbitration News Bulletin," *Trade/Commercial Arbitration/News* 1, November 1964, p. 30.

in the legal sense of the word, of the contracts giving rise to the disputes in question, can be realistic.

Sales/purchase contracts (wines, cereals, crude iron, iron ore, textiles, packing, machinery, ships, etc.)   30%

Commercial agency (pharmaceutical products, laboratory apparatus, printing-presses, chemical products, agricultural machinery, electrical equipment, etc.)   20%

Supply, and possibly installation, of industrial plant (works for treatment of coal, pumping installation, cement works, synthetic textile works, etc.)   15%

Licenses for patents, manufacturing processes, know-how, trademarks (treatment of textiles, manufacture of zip-fasteners, fountain pens, recording, scaffolding systems, moulding of plastic materials, manufacture of packing machines, anti-corrosive liquids, electric locomotives, etc.)   20%

Banking of financial operations (documentary credit, consequences of a monetary devaluation, formation of companies, transfer of debts, etc.)   8%

Miscellaneous   7%

For the total number of cases examined, the duration of arbitration may be broken down as follows: 50% of 6 to 12 months duration, 38% of 12 to 18 months duration, and 12% over 18 months.

ECAFE (Economic Commission for Asia and the Far East) Center for the Promotion of Commercial Arbitration. A rather conspicuous statistic in I.C.C.'s representation is the limited number of disputes it has arbitrated involving companies from either Africa or Asia. Possible explanations are many. Among them would be that the extent of international trade in this area is quite small compared with Europe and the United States. Another explanation, however, and one that seems to be increasingly significant, is that these countries and their nationals are not always eager to resort to tribunals that have been associated with Western trade and commerce over the years. As we have seen, I.C.C.'s list of arbitrators contained only two from Africa and Asia. One of the complicating features of international commercial arbitration is that the nationality of the arbitrators is a very sensitive aspect of the procedure. The very conditions that frequently result in misunderstanding and suspicion between nationals of different countries manifest themselves in a desire for an arbitrator from a third country.

This desire for a neutral arbitrator is particularly acute in those areas of the world where self-conscious nationalism constitutes such a significant force. Particularly in Asia and Africa it is consistent with political and economic beliefs to be reluctant to engage in international arbitration where the proceedings are conducted in a Western country and the arbitrator is of Western origin.

Such attitudes have led in recent years to attempts by the nations of Asia and the Far East, under the auspices of the United Nations agency ECAFE, to develop local arbitration facilities that could hear international disputes between their citizens and the Western world. In fact, this particular United Nations regional commission has instituted the ECAFE Center for the Promotion of Commercial Arbitration. A quotation from its first *News Bulletin* follows:

> The need to open up more practical channels for settling disputes arising from international trade and commerce is being increasingly felt, particularly by the developing countries of the ECAFE region which are now engaged in efforts to expand their international trade on a sustained basis. These countries are becoming increasingly aware that commercial arbitration facilities in the region are far from adequate and that more intensive efforts should be directed towards their improvement and at the establishment of new facilities.[13]

The positive statement of the commission tends to obscure the real reason for this intensive interest. One of the members of the commission reveals the real motivation when he says, "It is clear that the developing countries are not in favor of arbitration abroad. Nor are those abroad in favor of arbitration in developing countries." In fact, there is a plentiful supply of arbitration facilities in both Europe and the United States to handle the disputes. The simple fact, however, is that many countries in Asia are suspicious of Western institutions and probably tired of always being the party traveling to the arbitration site. On the other hand, Western commerce is understandably reluctant about putting the rather primitive state of certain Asian and Far Eastern arbitration tribunals to any test. India and Japan are rather notable exceptions to the relatively rudimentary state of arbitration which prevails throughout the region.

Currently, most of the Western firms engaged in commercial transactions in these areas have been able to wield their more powerful bargaining position in a way so as to avoid local arbitration. However, as these areas become more conscious of their potency and as their bargaining strength is increased, Western firms can expect pressure to use some

[13] *ECAFE News Bulletin, op. cit.,* p. 3.

form of regional arbitration facilities. We expect that the United Nations-sponsored efforts now under way will result in the development of more reliable traditions and institutions in the area. It certainly is not unreasonable to expect that panels of arbitrators and procedures suitable to all parties will eventually evolve. A somewhat analagous development has been the Inter-American Commercial Arbitration Commission, which has been able to evolve procedures and arbitrator lists that have proven satisfactory to both the underdeveloped and developed nations of the American continents.

World Bank Convention. A recent development in arbitration mechanisms is the Convention on the Settlement of Investment Disputes between States and Nationals of Other States announced March 18, 1965. This Convention is significant because its explicit purpose is to deal with those investment disputes that have proliferated in recent years primarily between Western investors and the governments of the underdeveloped nations. Of further significance, however, is the fact that the motivation for it came from an international agency—the International Bank for Reconstruction and Development (World Bank)—and participation in the administration of the institution will be by representatives of the respective governments that join.

The Convention itself authorizes the institution of the International Center for Settlement of Investment Disputes. Each country that signs the Convention contributes a representative to the administrative council of the Center. Its activities include adoption of rules of procedure for the institution of arbitration proceedings and adoption of rules of procedure for the arbitration proceedings, per se. Furthermore, each contracting state may designate to the panel of arbitrators four persons who may, but need not be, its nationals.

The nature and composition of the Center are such that member governments indirectly play an active role, both in the administrative council and in the selection of arbitrator panels. We saw traces of this governmental involvement in arbitration with the United Nations sponsored ECAFE Center for the Promotion of Commercial Arbitration. Nonetheless, both of these centers receive their support from international organizations which, in turn, receive their support from the governments of the world. This is an extremely interesting development in view of the fact that the governments of the world are becoming increasingly involved in those very commercial transactions that have strong potential for disputes.

The charter for the International Center specifically excludes all disputes other than those involving a state and an investor from another state. As such, it excludes a vast array of commercial disputes currently being arbitrated before other tribunals. The fact that each participating government can place four nationals on the panel of arbitrators will tend to obviate nationalistic fears of biased arbitrators that seem to be such a concern for the underdeveloped countries.

The preamble to the Convention states that "no contracting State shall by the mere fact of its ratification, acceptance or approval of this Convention and without its consent be deemed to be under an obligation to submit any particular dispute to arbitration." Although the government may sign the Convention, participate in the administrative council, and select arbitrators for the panel, it is not compelled to submit an investment dispute it may have with a foreign national to the arbitration of the Center. It is expected, however, that investors in the future may often insist on an advance commitment from the host country to submit disputes to the new arbitration procedure of the World Bank.

A final fact to be noted is that the Convention would not come into effect until it has been signed and ratified by 20 nations: "When the bank's board of governors instructed the executive directors last year in Tokyo to draw up the Convention, the Latin American countries and the Philippines voted against the resolution. However, officials were hopeful . . . that at least some Latin-American countries would sign it."[14] Considerable debate centers around the position that the United States will take. The United States refused to participate in either of the Geneva Conventions in the twenties and so far has refused to sign the United Nations Convention of 1958. However, there are several members of the U.S. Government that anticipate an affirmative action by the State Department.

It is true, of course, that conceptually there is considerable difference between past multilateral conventions on international arbitration and the current one proposed by the World Bank. The respective governments are not being asked to have their judiciaries accept as binding the arbitration proceedings in other nations regardless of under whose auspices they take place. This request is far more specific in nature; it concerns only those proceedings that are carried out under the jurisdiction of the Center. Furthermore, the Government will participate to some degree in the administration of the Center. There seems to be some hope, therefore, that the U. S. Government will become a signatory of the Convention.

Our belief is that a significant number of underdeveloped nations will

[14] *The New York Times,* March 30, 1965.

participate in the Convention. Although the submission of commercial disputes by sovereign governments to another party is not an extremely palatable undertaking, it may become a condition in securing foreign capital. If this is so, it would seem that these countries would far rather submit their disputes to such a quasi-public body than to the exclusively private tribunals which presently are in existence.

Noninstitutionalized arbitration. The final form of international commercial arbitration which we shall discuss is that which transpires on a noninstitutionalized basis. Ground rules, procedures, and arbitrators are all designated by the respective parties. This form of commercial arbitration has been most frequently used when one of the parties has been a government. Such arrangements have been worked out between several oil companies and Middle East governments. Usually, the arbitrator is someone of impeccable reputation, quite frequently associated with the International Court of Justice.

The disadvantages of this type of arbitration reside in the difficulties of autonomously constructing arbitration procedures and ground rules for each potential dispute. The advantages of institutionalized arbitration are that the procedures and mechanism of the tribunal are widely publicized, predictable, and easily utilized. These attributes all contrast with the burdensome requisites of noninstitutionalized arbitration. Predictability and traditional behavior are cornerstones in any process of adjudication. Once the decision has been made to employ arbitration, we believe that businessmen should look toward recognized and respected arbitration tribunals, rather than toward improvisation of ad hoc arbitration procedures.

CURRENT ATTITUDES OF BUSINESS COMMUNITY TOWARD INTERNATIONAL COMMERCIAL ARBITRATION

As we have seen, a necessary antecedent for the frequent use of international commercial arbitration is the mutual trust and confidence among businessmen, both in the competence of the arbitrators and in the procedures and regulations of the arbitration proceedings. This trust is most conveniently fostered by the establishment of institutionalized tribunals with widely known and acceptable rules of operation.

Earlier we noted the unique pressures in international commerce that make the arbitration site a contentious and critical element of the international arbitration process. Unlike domestic commerce, there is no one geographical site that will satisfy all the nationals of the commercial world.

Increasingly, it is being required that arbitration traditions and facilities be established in more than one area, particularly as trade patterns become more dispersed and "international" in character. The ECAFE development is, of course, a notable example of such an international force at work.

In recognition of this need for arbitration facilities, it is particularly significant to note that 88 percent of our questionnaire respondents believed that "more widely recognized international arbitration tribunals would facilitate the use of arbitration procedures by international traders." Furthermore, a significant number made the positive assertion that insufficient arbitration facilities hindered the acceptance of arbitration practices.

This attitude on the part of the U.S. international businessman imparts an element of urgency to those efforts to institute arbitration procedures and facilities in the underdeveloped areas of the world.

To ascertain the degree to which the U.S. international business community is familiar with international commercial arbitration, we devised a "scale of familiarity" numbered from one to ten (ten = complete familiarity). The tabulation of these rather subjective inputs revealed that among manufacturers one-third were "completely familiar," one-third were "moderately familiar," and one-third were "relatively unfamiliar" with international arbitration. Among traders (export-import middlemen), 100 percent checked number five or above on our scale. The bankers seemed to indicate that they were even more familiar with arbitration procedures than were the traders.

The overall picture resulting from this rather impressionistic survey is that the international commercial community quite probably has a significantly greater familiarity with international commercial arbitration than do domestic counterparts with the process of domestic commercial arbitration.

The probable reasons for this heightened awareness stem from two interrelated phenomena. First, we have seen that historically it has been from the international area that commercial arbitration has received its primary impetus. Second, the theme of this chapter has been that businessmen engaged in international commerce must be extremely cognizant of potentials for dispute. We have been developing the premise that arbitration is the most satisfactory vehicle for settling many of these disputes. It is certainly reasonable to expect that businessmen, in confirmation of these differentiating characteristics, should possess a more acute awareness internationally than domestically of arbitration facilities.

Sixty-five percent of the total questionnaire respondents believed commercial arbitration to be more suitable internationally than domestically. There were two primary reasons cited for this belief. First, the respondents believed the great importance of continuing relations in international commerce dramatically highlighted the advantages of arbitration with respect to both speed and preservation of business rapport. Second, they believed that the problems of interstate enforcement of commercial adjudication were not nearly so severe as the problems of internation enforcement. Therefore, any enforcement advantages that arbitration has to offer are more relevant internationally than domestically.

One hundred percent of the responding exporters and importers used the international commercial arbitration clause in their purchase-sale contracts. The acceptance of arbitration by this group seems to validate the conclusions developed in our previous section on purchase-sale contracts. Not unexpectedly, the traders unanimously agreed that arbitration was more suitable for international situations than for domestic transactions.

One hundred percent of the responding traders preferred international commercial arbitration to court litigation. A sampling of their reasons for this preference follows.

- Leaves door open for further business transactions.
- More expedient.
- Matter under dispute is considered by persons who are familiar with the commodity or trade involved; faster decision rendered.
- Quicker, to the point, and no technical delays and misinterpretation.

These reasons, of course, are reiterations of the advantages of arbitration that have been cited in previous sections and chapters. It is especially significant that this particular group of businessmen, faced as they are with small margins and entirely dependent upon continuity of trade relations, should so overwhelmingly prefer and utilize arbitration.

Of the manufacturers responding to our questionnaire, 72 percent have used arbitration clauses in their international commercial contracts. These clauses included the entire spectrum of transactions: purchase-sale, licensing, investment protection, and joint venture. In view of this seeming acceptance of arbitration, it is surprising that, when asked about their preference between arbitration and litigation, 50 percent of the manufacturers favored litigation.

Our explanation for this apparent incongruity is that the foreign trading partners of these manufacturers in many instances insisted upon the inclusion of an arbitration clause as part of the terms of the contract. In fact, one of the respondents specifically said, "It has been our experience that the foreign . . . parties with whom we contract prefer in most instances the use of arbitration instead of court action." This tends to confirm our supposition that arbitration is more intensively utilized abroad than in the United States.

Further evidence of a tendency for foreign nationals to exercise their preference for arbitration through contract negotiations is evidenced by one company that stated, "[we] use . . . arbitration normally only if customer insists. . . ." Another firm noted that some of "our formal contracts with purchasers of our products and services, including foreign governments, and with licensees and others, do, however, contain arbitration provisions as a result of the contract negotiations." It is interesting that neither of these respondents preferred arbitration. Yet they adopted it at the insistence of the foreign party.

Furthermore, the attitude of the manufacturers toward the question of litigation versus international commercial arbitration was directly traceable to the legal advice which they had received. As we have indicated in previous chapters, the American legal fraternity has been reticent in recommending arbitration to the businessman as a dispute-settling tool. Yet the contract negotiations between foreign and U.S. businessmen have resulted in considerable arbitration usage. The exigencies of business have superseded the advisories of the legal community.

We have contrasted the traders' 100 percent preference for international commercial arbitration to the manufacturers' considerably less enthusiastic preference. There could be several reasons for this rather significant disparity. Of critical importance is the fact that export-import middlemen, for the most part, take part in only purchase-sale contracts. Historically, we saw that it was to this type of transaction that international arbitration was first applied. Manufacturers, on the other hand, face a significantly broader spectrum of contractual arrangements. The increased complexity of these contracts requires more arbitral skill than do quality- and product-oriented purchase-sale disputes.

General-purpose arbitration tribunals with the competence to adjudicate these types of disputes have not come into full prominence until recent decades. On the other hand, trade association tribunals have existed for centuries. It is only natural, therefore, that manufacturers faced with complex licensing disputes should be less enthusiastic about arbitration than those traders who encounter disputes that international commercial arbitration has successfully processed for centuries.

The vast majority of export-importers revealed that their advice to utilize arbitration facilities came not from the legal profession but from the trade associations. Manufacturers, on the other hand, received their advice from the legal community. Much of the difference in arbitration attitudes on the part of these two business groups can probably be traced to their differing sources of advice.

A final explanation of the disparity seems to reside in the attitude prevalent on the part of some businessmen that arbitration signifies "compromise" rather than adjudicating what is "right" and what is "wrong." The international vice president of a large steel producer spoke about "the tendency in arbitration to seek a compromise position; and frequent confusion as to whether the arbitration is confined to legal right or whether equity and 'other considerations' will be relevant." A large producer of automobiles "considered 'legal rights' better protected in litigation."

Manufacturers with well-established legal divisions might be able to afford to worry about the assurance of justice and the prevention of compromise. The traders, on the other hand, with fewer lawyers and less time at their disposal, unanimously resorted to the less costly and the less time-consuming arbitration tribunals.

The fact must not be obscured, however, that 50 percent of these large manufacturers stated unequivocally that they preferred international commercial arbitration to litigation. We have presented below a sampling of the reasons for their preferences:

- Less nationalistic.
- Simplicity of procedure.
- Quicker, certainty of reaching decision.
- Greater convenience and preservation of relations with customer.
- Better prospects of amicable settlement.

Eighty-two percent of all manufacturing respondents, regardless of whether they generally preferred arbitration to litigation, mentioned that international commercial arbitration can be useful in licensing agreements, foreign investment contracts, and agreements with foreign governments. In fact, they indicated that these types of transactions were more amenable to international arbitration than were export-import, purchase-sale agreements. The explanation for this is twofold. First, large domestic manufacturers are doing increasingly less exporting and importing. Manufacturers are now expanding their productive organization abroad to meet the foreign requirements, thus raising the incidence of foreign subsidiary investment and decreasing the amount of exports and imports. Second, as general-purpose arbitration tribunals have become better staffed and more institutionalized, the business community has increasingly realized the relevance of arbitration for these more complex types of transactions. Even more than the product-oriented quality and delivery disputes, licensing and investment disputes highlight the extra-legal advantages which arbitration has to offer. If the arbitrators are equal to the task, circumvention of legal procedures in licensing procedures pays even more dividends in time saved and costs averted.

Of the international bankers who responded to our questionnaire, 100 percent agreed that arbitration was more suitable internationally than domestically. There was also 100-percent agreement that international commercial arbitration was preferable to litigation. Eighty percent listed as their reason that it was "quicker and less costly."

This rather surprising endorsement serves as a useful conclusion to this subsection on international dispute mechanisms. We have found that there were questionnaire responses that recommended, in one form or another, all the general types of dispute-settling mechanisms that have been discussed. Yet it is quite clear that of all the third-party procedures, arbitration received the most consistent endorsement by the widest segment of the U.S. business community.

ENFORCEMENT OF INTERNATIONAL ADJUDICATION

The enforceability of the decision rendered in an international commercial dispute is a vital, perhaps *the most* vital, ingredient in a decision as to which type of adjudication to seek. Except in those instances when an industry tribunal can rely upon the effective internal policing powers of a cohesive trade association, this enforcement must be provided by the legal arm of the respective government.

In a way, it is presumptuous of us to attempt to deal with a topic that is as complex and indeterminate as this one is at the present time. Legal experts differ, and assertions on this topic seem to be valid only until a relevant case emerges somewhere in the world to contradict them. Inasmuch as answers, tentative as they may be, to this critical question of international enforceability must be provided, we will attempt to summarize and restate the positions that presently seem to represent a consensus among those conversant with the issues. By no means, however, should this summarization be construed as either definitive or immutable.

The following two quotations will provide a useful beginning to the discussion:

> Arbitral awards, following the Geneva Convention, have been more freely enforceable throughout the world than judicial decision. The explanation

is that lawyers of the past generation have considered awards the outcome of contractual relationships, rather than of the exercise of state powers. . . . . The exaggerated respect for state power and state sovereignty in this field have brought about a loss in the importance of power and sovereignty alike.[15]

One foreign legal system is even more suspicious of another foreign judgment than of an arbitral award. This suspicion is based on the concept that the arbitral award is not, after all, an act of a state, but is based on the will of the parties.[16]

To say that foreign arbitral awards are "more freely enforceable throughout the world than judicial decision," is quite obviously a relative assertion. "More freely . . . than" does not tell us that arbitral awards can with certainty be enforced throughout the world. Professor Habscheid is even less optimistic. The edge he gives to arbitration is of a most decidedly negative nature. Legal systems are less suspicious of arbitral awards than of foreign judgments. Indeed, there is a significant gap between "less suspicious of" and certainty regarding award enforcement.

Given the general premise, however, that arbitration affords the businessman a better chance of foreign enforcement than does litigation, let us examine some of the specifics of internation arbitration enforcement. Dr. Martin Domke, an acknowledged expert and authority on international commercial arbitration, quotes from an American Law Institute publication:

Foreign arbitration awards have been enforced almost invariably in the United States provided that (1) they were enforceable in the state of their rendition, (2) the cause of action on which they were based was not contrary to the strong public policy of the forum and (3) either the defendant or his property was subject to the judicial jurisdiction of the arbitration tribunal and the defendant was given reasonable notice of the proceeding and a reasonable opportunity to be heard.[17]

In a recent statement given to the authors, Dr. Domke elaborated on the subject of internation arbitration enforcement:

Enforcement of a foreign award is moreover possible only by an order of

[15] E. J. Cohn, "Economic Integration and International Commercial Arbitration," in M. Domke (ed.), *International Trade Arbitration* (New York: American Arbitration Association, 1958), p. 21.

[16] W. J. Habscheid, "Unification in the Enforcement of Foreign Awards," in M. Domke (ed.), *International Trade Arbitration* (New York: American Arbitration Association, 1958), p. 199.

[17] M. Domke, *International Arbitration of Commercial Disputes* (a pamphlet), p. 152. Reprinted from *The Proceedings of the 1960 Institute on Private Investments Abroad*. Quoting from: American Law Institute. Restatement of the Law Second. Conflict of Laws. Tentative Draft No. 6, of April 22, 1960.

the competent judicial authority which would have to investigate not the merits of the American award but the compliance with the requirements of the law of the country where enforcement is being sought. Enforcement of American awards has taken place in Columbia (1950), England (1952), Switzerland (1955), Philippines (1957), Brazil (1958), Germany (1959), and France (1963).

A rather startling point in this regard is made by Ernest Mezger, a French attorney:

> Contrary to wide-spread opinion, a so-called domestic or national arbitration award is subject to more intensive examination and is consequently more vulnerable, in most countries, to a refusal of recognition and execution than is a so-called foreign award. Under French law, e.g., a domestic award is subject to appeal, whereas a foreign award cannot be appealed from.[18]

It appears not only that foreign arbitral awards are more enforceable than foreign court judgments but also that foreign arbitral awards may be more enforceable than domestic awards. This latter point, however, is probably less true than the former when tested against the broad spectrum of national legal attitudes. Within the United States, for instance, it is probably not true.

One of the disadvantages that U.S. businessmen face regarding foreign award enforcement, vis-à-vis their foreign counterpart, is that the United States Government has not been a signatory to any of the multilateral conventions concerning arbitration. To varying degrees, these conventions have facilitated the task of foreign award enforcement. However, there are two factors that contribute to the current situation wherein one can reasonably expect enforcement both abroad and domestically. First, there are the Friendship, Commerce, and Navigation Treaties that have been concluded since World War II with 15 foreign nations. These treaties provide a negative protection that, in effect, precludes discrimination against an award just because it emanated from a foreign arbitrator or a foreign situs of the arbitration proceedings. The practical effect in this country is that foreign awards are afforded the same judicial treatment as domestic awards.

The second factor involves the judicial concept of comity between national judiciaries. It is in effect a gentleman's agreement, not a right, that permits enforcement of a foreign award from Country *B* to Country *A* if Country *B* would, in turn, have enforced an award from Country *A*.

[18] E. Mezger, "The Arbitrator and Private International Law," in M. Domke (ed.), *International Trade Arbitration* (New York: American Arbitration Association, 1958), p. 230.

Insofar as the United States is generally willing to enforce foreign arbitral awards subject to the preconditions cited by Dr. Domke above, there has evolved a reasonably predictable situation insofar as enforcement of arbitration awards involving the United States is concerned.

These scattered, almost makeshift legal practices, have resulted in a surprising degree of internation enforceability for arbitral awards. The businessman of a country whose government fails to participate in multilateral conventions attempting to insure uniform enforceability can expect to find, nevertheless, that his contractual arrangements to arbitrate will be respected and enforced by most national judiciaries.

International commercial arbitration, therefore, has an impressive array of advantages to recommend it as a dispute-settling mechanism. Most significant of all the attributes is that there is a greater likelihood of foreign award enforcement than foreign judgment enforcement. It is the opinion of the authors that in most instances international commercial arbitration in all its many facets and forms constitutes a most usable and workable dispute-settling tool for the international businessman.

CONCLUSIONS AND PREDICTION FOR THE FUTURE

A consistent theme running throughout this chapter has been that international commercial arbitration is a useful procedure by which disputes arising from many types of international transactions can be adjudicated and enforced.

International arbitration presents even more compelling opportunities vis-à-vis corresponding legal systems than does its domestic counterpart. This situation arises both from an aggravation of those factors that encourage arbitration domestically and from barriers and constraints unique with international transactions.

Arbitration awards afford the businessman a mechanism by which the debilitating forces of legalistic sovereignty can be circumvented. Even though the United States Government has not participated in any of the multilateral conventions dealing with the issue of internation enforceability, we saw in the preceding section that the U.S. businessman can still anticipate a significant degree of internation enforceability of arbitration awards.

There are three basic means by which the problems of enforcing international commercial judgments and awards can be formally confronted. If *litigation* is preferred, there could be an attempt to standardize and unify the respective commercial statutes and commercial laws among the national judiciaries of the world. Such uniformity might then lead to predictable recognition, whether explicitly achieved through multilateral conventions or implicitly achieved through rigorous reciprocity of commercial judgments throughout the various national legal systems of the world.

The problems of such an approach are numerous. Consolidation of national statutes and laws, even in an area as specialized as commercial and contract law, presents significant obstacles. Concomitant with this difficulty is the traditional notion of legal sovereignty that will undoubtedly result in significant resistance even where some degree of statute uniformity has been achieved. Such a resolution to the problem of internation enforcement of commercial adjudication is not likely to be obtained in the near future.

A second approach to the problem would be to vitalize a *multilateral arbitral convention,* such as the New York (United Nations) Convention of 1958. Such an approach is decidedly more feasible. Rather than unifying the commercial statutes, per se, the attempt would be to unify the formalized recognition which the respective national judiciaries have given to the extra-legal arbitral process.

It requires only a brief statute or precedent to constitute and legitimize the arbitration process in a given country. This simplicity stands in rather sharp contrast to the maze of national statutes and precedents that attend the litigation of commercial disputes in the courts of the national judiciaries. It would seem to be a far easier task to unify the respective arbitration statutes among nations than to unify their respective commercial law statutes and precedents.

The increasing development of arbitration practice among the businessmen of the world and the legitimation of such activities by their respective nation states have already fostered the development, in an informal fashion, of some degree of uniformity among the various national arbitration statutes.

The arbitral process is, to be sure, legitimatized and constituted by the respective national judiciaries. However, the process seems to be viewed by foreign judiciaries more as the right of two private parties to the freedom of contract than as a proceeding sanctioned by another sovereign legal system.

In contrast, securing enforceability through litigation would encounter not only the unification problem but also the rather difficult and intangible problem of how to deal with sovereignty considerations that pervade national judiciaries. Political and legal history both suggest that there will always be some reluctance by national judiciaries in enforcing, a priori, the judgments of foreign judiciaries upon domestic nationals.

As was mentioned earlier, 29 nations have already acceded to the New York Convention on the Recognition and Enforcement of Foreign Arbitral Awards. In 1960 the American Bar Association came out forcefully for U.S. participation in the Convention. Although the United States has yet to sign, we believe the prospects for eventual U.S. participation are good. For the reasons developed above, we believe that a multilateral convention is a feasible route by which to insure internation enforcement of arbitral awards.

The final approach which can be taken to secure internation enforceability of the adjudication of commercial disputes is contained within the recent *World Bank proposal* to institute the International Center for Settlement of Investment Disputes. Government signatories to the enabling Convention would be instituting a specific arbitral mechanism in which they would have equal voice in administration of the Center and in development of arbitrator lists. Rather than providing for the recognition of awards rendered in foreign countries, as does the New York Convention, the World Bank Convention actually sets up an international arbitral mechanism. The difference is quite significant. The World Bank Convention does not require the domestic judiciary to enforce awards rendered under the aegis of any foreign judiciary whose government happened to be a signatory to the New York Convention. It obligates the domestic judiciary to recognize and enforce only the awards rendered by the Center to which, in turn, the domestic government has the privilege of belonging.

On this question of enforcement, there is no doubt. Article 54 of the World Bank Convention specifically states, "Each Contracting State shall recognize an award rendered pursuant to this Convention as binding and enforce the pecuniary obligations imposed by that award within its territories as if it were a final judgment of a court in that State." Its aim is the ultimate goal of all internation enforcement attempts: domestic treatment as if the arbitration award were a final judgment of the domestic courts.

It is the authors' belief that institutions such as this, created with public sanction and support, will provide the greatest contribution to international commercial arbitration in the years to come. This approach would seem to circumvent more successfully than the New York Convention the suspicions which national judiciaries have of one another. It is true that awards rendered by a supranational body would be substituted for awards rendered by arbitral processes under the aegis of foreign judiciaries. It is our belief, however, that in commercial disputes the world's governments would be more willing to curtail their legal sovereignty on the behalf of an international center to which they belong than on the behalf of all the foreign judiciaries of the world.

Such a trend would have significant implications for the current private trade and general-purpose arbitral tribunals. Their role in international commercial arbitration would thereby be reduced. Private organizations such as the American Arbitration Association and the International Chamber of Commerce would obviously be affected. Although present World Bank proposals limit the jurisdiction of the Center to only investment disputes involving a government and a foreign national, there is no reason why the scope of World Bank's proposals could not be expanded to include a broader spectrum of dispute contingencies—broader both as to transaction and party.

Finally, we would note that such publicly sponsored arbitration tribunals would offer advantages in addition to the facilitation of internation award enforcement. As we discussed earlier, certain areas of the world have serious reservations about participation in private tribunals that have been evolved over the years to meet the needs of Western industry and commerce. Without speculating on the legitimacy of their contentions, it seems clear that publicly sponsored tribunals such as the Center would be considerably more acceptable to both their governments and their businessmen. Furthermore, one suspects that state-owned economic entities would also prefer to arbitrate under the aegis of an institution to which the government of the country belongs.

We also anticipate further arbitration interest on the part of regional United Nations economic commissions, such as ECAFE. There are indications that ECAFE is thinking in terms of active participation in the processes of Far East international commercial arbitration. There have already been preliminary suggestions that the ECAFE Center for the Promotion of Commercial Arbitration provide arbitration services such as formulating arbitrator lists and actually selecting arbitrators for the disputants. We view such developments as an extension of the trend toward increasing utilization and institution of publicly sponsored and supported arbitration facilities.

A change of this nature would certainly please those contemporary critics who view private arbitration proceedings and prerogatives as unregulated cartelization of commercial power. The institution of such public participation and interest should mitigate the dangers of such private power concentrations. Having circumvented the jurisdiction of domestic judiciaries, the disputants would once again appear under the auspices of public adjudication.

CHAPTER VII

THE FUTURE OF
COMMERCIAL ARBITRATION •

The COMMERCIAL ARBITRATION PROCESS is not well known in, or properly appreciated by, the business community today. Most businessmen have never heard of it. To those businessmen who are intimately familiar with the rituals and results of labor arbitration, it is often "that other kind of arbitration."

WHERE WE ARE TODAY

There are a few organizations doing missionary work in the field. The American Arbitration Association, under its able president, Donald Straus, is making an intensive effort to increase the general knowledge concerning commercial arbitration. In the international area, a similar effort is being made by the International Chamber of Commerce and by agencies of the United Nations. But, to an extent, they are all voices crying out in the wilderness. The businessman is not going to turn his attention to commercial arbitration as long as he considers it to be the strict province of his attorney and until he sees economic advantage in doing so. Trade group arbitration is an exception to this generalization, but the focus of trade groups is internal. They are not usually concerned with the uses of commercial arbitration outside their own areas of operation.

The interest of attorneys in commercial arbitration is growing. The historic hostility of the courts to the arbitration tribunal has diminished in the face of increasingly crowded calendars and pressures for speedier justice. New decisions affirming the irrevocability of the agreement to arbitrate have been rendered, and modern statutes removing arbitration from the governance of the common law have been passed in 21 states. Lawyer participation in commercial arbitration is tending to cause the process to become increasingly legalistic in nature. This trend is viewed with alarm by some and with pleasure by others.

Many attorneys and jurists remain suspicious of commercial arbitration, contending that private systems of justice represent concentrations of power which can be misused. Others cannot accept the suspension of such legal safeguards as the rules of evidence, adherence to precedent, and the right of appeal. Still others believe that the inclusion in a contract of a general arbitration clause causes commercial arbitration to encroach upon areas in which it is admittedly not appropriate.

Certain businessmen criticize arbitration on the basis that it is not a forum for factual decision but rather a method of compromise. Almost half the arbitrators surveyed in the course of this research agree that the result of their decision is compromise. However, the research has uncovered two meanings of the word compromise. The majority of those reporting use it to mean the determination of a correct position somewhere between two extreme views. A few employ it in its invidious sense of "splitting the difference."

Commercial arbitration is used in a diversity of ways in order to resolve a variety of disputes. However, these uses are occasional and isolated. The American Arbitration Association attempts to operate as a central clearinghouse for the uses of commercial arbitration, but many businessmen view the association as overly parochial and treat the information accordingly. Other discussions of arbitration appear in arcane law journals; while they may inspire interest on the part of attorneys, they are never seen by businessmen.

The general acceptance and expanded use of commercial arbitration is contingent upon the establishment of a viable accommodation between businessmen and attorneys. Acting alone, the attorney is prone to consider the process in terms of arbitration versus litigation and to change it in ways that he thinks would make it more palatable to other attorneys. Ultimately, arbitration could be suffocated in a legalistic embrace. On the other hand, if the businessman chooses to attempt to operate the mechanism apart from the attorney, it is unlikely that he would succeed. Even in the trade association where, to a degree, the businessman has been successful in accomplishing this exclusion of attorneys, there must exist some separate element of external compulsion, such as the absolute necessity for continuity of relationships, in order to make arbitration effective. Either the exigencies of a particular form of business or the force of law is required to insure that both parties will abide by an original agreement to arbitrate. When neither compulsion is present, it seems realistic to anticipate that the party who views his case as being the weaker of the two will find reasons to invalidate his commitment. In addition, we might speculate that the legal fraternity will militate against any exclusion and will raise the cry of private law and cartel discipline until they are permitted to participate. The amendment to the Civil Practices Act in New York State which prohibits general exclusion of attorneys as spokesmen for participants is a case in point. An awakened business community would probably not desire to remove the members of the Bar from a position of influence over the arbitration process in the future. However, an awakened business community would balance such influence and offset the creeping legalism that threatens to remove economic practicality from the process.

FACTORS INFLUENCING FUTURE USE OF COMMERCIAL ARBITRATION

Acceptance by attorneys. There is little doubt that commercial arbitration will survive in some form. The evidence to be adduced from Chapter V is that, if anything, the problem of court congestion will grow rather than diminish. Furthermore, there are indications that as more attorneys become familiar with commercial arbitration, their hostility will subside. There is even an argument that attorneys may find the practice of arbitration economically rewarding:

> The attorney unfamiliar with arbitration, but aware that it is a fast and economical method of resolving disputes, may feel that the practice of arbitration is a financially unrewarding one. This is not true. If we denigrate the American lawyer by characterizing him as a person solely interested in financial reward and not at all interested in public service, we could say for that reason attorneys should avoid arbitration. It is a fact, however, that arbitration not only serves a necessary public good, but also has material rewards.

Lionel S. Popkin, a New York attorney, has stated the case as follows:

"Arbitration benefits the lawyer—have no doubt about that. The lawyer's time is saved and his convenience is served by arbitration. There is no time-consuming procedure of attending calendar calls, waiting for the previous case to be finished, picking juries, and preliminary motions and appeals. The fee of the lawyers in arbitration not only is at a much higher rate for the time actually spent, as opposed to court actions, but generally is as much in dollars and cents. The disposition of an arbitration in a comparatively short time assures the lawyer that the evidence and witnesses will be available, that a debtor will not have the usual lengthy period while a court action is pending to dispose of his assets and prevent collection of the claim, and that the controversy will be disposed of quickly and the lawyer's fee paid."[1]

There seems little reason to believe that the involvement of the attorney with commercial arbitration will decrease.

State statutes and commercial arbitration. Although we have no specific evidence to substantiate the point, it is reasonable to believe that as the national volume of trade increases and as new trading areas come into being, more states will consider the adoption of modern arbitration statutes.

Some of the businessmen and attorneys we interviewed speculated that other factors would also influence such adoption. For example:

- Because of the increase in accident cases, the insurance lobby is supporting the uniform arbitration law more vigorously.
- The local bar associations recognize that not having a modern law results in the handling of arbitrations in more hospitable states—for example, in New York, California, Illinois.
- National businesses are impatient with local state laws. They desire a national system of jurisprudence, and their agitation could affect the future of arbitration.

Acceptance by businessmen. The future of commercial arbitration depends to a very great extent on whether or not the business community sees enough value in commercial arbitration to make an effort toward preserving its business-oriented characteristics. The principal factors affecting the future use of commercial arbitration are business-oriented. The new technology has produced a degree of complexity in business relationships that could not have been envisioned 15 years ago. The growth of the economy has turned many corporations into super-giants, and they have become painfully conscious about size. These two factors seem to be having a similar effect. In one case, the nature of potential disputes is so

---

[1] Abraham A. Diamond, "The Process of Arbitration," *Chicago Bar Record,* Volume XLVI, November 2, November 1964, p. 77. (Quoting Lionel S. Popkin, "Practical Problems Confronting the Practical Lawyer," *Law and Contemporary Problems,* Vol. 17, No. 4, Autumn 1952, p. 652.)

infinitely complex that the presence of an expert is almost imperative for their solution. In the other, business is searching for ways to demonstrate that it can be statesmanlike rather than predatory.

There is great potential advantage in creating an arbitration-conditioned environment. The most significant lesson to be learned from the experience of the New York Stock Exchange and many of the trade associations is that as arbitration becomes better understood it is less frequently employed. The simple discipline of arbitration evidently sharpens the ability and the desire to negotiate and, at the same time, removes any advantage that might have been found in procrastination. A Minneapolis attorney writes:

> . . . I have had occasion to include arbitration provisions in contracts involving valuation questions on purchase and sale of real estate and of businesses, especially where the option date or exchange date is some years in the future. We have tended to provide for a third arbitrator to be selected by the local state district court. I would say that we have not needed to use these arbitration provisions, but their presence undoubtedly has aided amicable handling of the subsequent valuations. . . .

Most significant is the vast potential of the international arena, and the realization on the part of more and more businessmen that they must think in terms of a world market. The differences among national legal systems will not be reconciled in the near future. It seems likely that as the volume of international trade increases, so will the number of disputes.

The area of international commercial arbitration, as discussed in the preceding chapter, is similar to but far more complex than domestic arbitration. In some ways arbitration is even more applicable in the international situation. There is every reason to believe that the use of international arbitration will expand. Multinational agreements, specialized mechanisms such as the World Bank's investment arbitration, and other forms will, in all likelihood, be employed to a far greater extent than any proposed form of supranational litigation. The problems of jealousy over sovereignty and economic nationalism will remain and become even more complex as new nations continue along the cycle of their emergence. This is all the more reason for the American businessman to get off the sideline and into the game. The businessman may find himself with the choice of becoming embroiled in international arbitration either as a sponsor or as a stranger. Therefore, the businessman should be strongly motivated to have a voice in the evolution of, and to participate in, the mechanisms of international trade arbitration.

Acceptance by educators. The involvement of businessmen and the attitudes of attorneys depend to a large extent on the treatment given to the process of commercial arbitration by the educational community. Currently, this treatment is either nonexistent or minimal. The survey of the deans of 75 law schools and graduate schools of business administration, which was cited in Chapters I and IV, indicated that the subject was taught in only 19 schools (13 law, 6 business), and the amount of time devoted to commercial arbitration averaged 1.3 hours a semester. There are indications that, in some areas, this amount of time is decreasing. The dean of a law school in the Rocky Mountain area wrote:

> From one viewpoint, we have taken a backward step in education on the subject of commercial arbitration. In past years one professor devoted approximately ten out of sixty hours of the Contracts course to this subject. His interests have led him into other fields, and currently the subject receives a scant hour in Contracts and perhaps another in Remedies.

However, the general view is far more optimistic. Out of 43 responses[2] received, 33 were in the form of letters, and many of these letters incorporated informed attitudes toward and predictions concerning arbitration.

In response to the question "In view of the crowded court calendars in many localities do you see any expanded use of the arbitration mechanism in the future?" 49 percent answered yes, 21 percent answered no, and 30 percent remained uncommitted.

In response to the question "Do you envision any changes in the curricula of law and business schools in order to provide attorneys and businessmen with a more adequate background on the subject?" 19 percent answered yes, 30 percent answered no, 26 percent remained uncommitted, and the remainder offered qualifications.

The principal argument of these qualifications was that there existed an active competition for curriculum time at both law and business schools and unless there was an active protagonist fighting for a course in commercial arbitration, it was unlikely that one would be created. Respondents reported that course materials were sadly lacking.[3] Four law schools suggested that the subject be treated more extensively in the business school, and one business school suggested that law schools ought to do more about it.

---

[2] Included schools in the following states: Alabama, Arkansas, California (3), Delaware, Florida, Georgia, Idaho, Illinois, Indiana, Iowa (2), Kansas, Kentucky, Maryland, Michigan (2), Minnesota (2), Missouri, New Jersey, New Mexico, New York (3), North Carolina, Ohio, Oklahoma (2), Oregon, Pennsylvania, Tennessee, Texas, Washington (2), West Virginia, Wisconsin (2), Wyoming.

[3] One respondent reports that Professor Bernstein at Yale is preparing such material. Dr. Martin Domke of the American Arbitration Association is also preparing a casebook.

A number of the schools which anticipated no curriculum change regretted the fact. Professor Sam Kagel of the University of California School of Law submitted this statement:

> I cannot say that I envision any changes in the curricula of law and business schools in order to provide attorneys and businessmen with a more adequate background in the use of commercial arbitration. The difficulty seems to be that many members of the faculties of such schools are themselves not familiar with the use and practice of commercial arbitration. Of course in my opinion there should be changes in the curricula of law and business schools to provide for education and training in the use of this technique.

Universities in Tennessee, West Virginia, and Iowa report the potential introduction of new courses in the subject in 1966 or 1967. The absolute amount of education which deals with the subject of commercial arbitration appears to be increasing slightly.

Advisory arbitration. It is conceivable that arbitration will serve a very useful purpose in the future by operating solely in an advisory capacity.

> . . . there is no reason why arbitration machinery cannot be used to obtain an advisory determination. For instance, the American Arbitration Association recently administered an advisory case in which two charities contested how the proceeds of a public fund drive should be allocated. Neither organization felt that it could legally bind itself in advance to the terms of the determination, so they mutually agreed that the award would be "advisory." But when the award was rendered, both charities abided by its terms. . . .[4]

There are many situations in which a party may be unable to bind itself to accept an arbitral decision but, at the same time, may sincerely desire an impartial adjudication. This is particularly true in the case of an agent acting for an organization as in the case of the charities described above. Even governments which in many cases are restricted by the terms of appropriation legislation from binding themselves to accept arbitral decision might find advisory arbitration attractive. Such a policy could save the government considerable expense in obviating the necessity for the maintenance of extensive internal investigatory and arbitration machinery. Advisory arbitration would also pertain to the problem cited by the Secretary of a Wisconsin paper company:

> The one possible area where we would certainly be most anxious to receive a decision expeditiously is that involving governmental regulatory agencies;

[4] Robert Coulson, "Management Arbitration in Action," *American Business Law Journal*, Volume 3, Number 4, Winter 1965.

for example, traffic hearings, settling of rates, granting of permits, and so forth. I have never heard of this as a possible area . . . and there may be statutory compelling reasons why this would not be possible, but I do feel that where there is a conflict between a governmental agency and an industry it would be beneficial to all concerned to have a disinterested, impartial arbitrator decide rather than the agency acting as prosecutor and judge.

SOME UNRESOLVED ISSUES

Standardization. Should arbitration procedures be standardized? In order to determine the major differences and similarities among arbitration systems throughout the country, a questionnaire was developed by a group of organizations which included: the arbitration committee of the Association of the Bar of the City of New York; the Commercial Arbitration Committee of the Section of Corporation, Banking and Business Law of the American Bar Association; the American Society of Association Executives; the American Arbitration Association; and the authors.

The questionnaire was distributed to 1,671 association executives, and 383 replies were received. Fifty-three associations reported that they employed commercial arbitration to settle disputes; of these, 18 refer to the rules of the American Arbitration Association with or without modifications. The remaining 35 represent a variety of procedures.

The accompanying table reflects the variety of procedures employed in trade-association arbitration. With the possible exception that 75 percent report that they require no administrative fee, this exhibit reveals no particular trend toward commonality. It is difficult to make a judgment as to which procedures are "superior." In all likelihood, each association has tailored its procedures to suit its own needs. The impetus for standardization would probably come from the legalists who see the need for tighter rules of evidence, written reasoned awards, and adherence to precedent whenever arbitration occurs.

Aside from this pressure and the fact that a standardized procedure would facilitate the mobility among tribunals of certain participants, there seems little reason to seek a standardized and uniform version of commercial arbitration.

Modification. It would seem to be in the best interests of all participants to conceive of arbitration not as opposed to litigation but as an adjunct to it. Several attorneys have suggested that it would be of considerable advantage if pretrial discovery proceedings were to be conducted through arbitration with the judgment being thereafter brought to litigation as a stipulation of the parties. If arbitration is to recast its image in the minds of many

PROCEDURAL VARIETY IN TRADE ASSOCIATIONS

The following table of questionnaire responses indicates the variety of trade association procedures now in effect:

Arbitrators selected by:	Association	49%
	Parties	32
Arbitrators compensated:	Yes	36%
	Expenses only	14
	No	50
Number of arbitrators on panel:	Fixed	65%
	Variable	35
Arbitrators required to state reasons for their decision:	Yes	46%
	No	54
An appeal mechanism is available:	Yes	47%
	No	53
Jurisdiction obtained by:	Contract clause	37%
	Voluntary submission	40
	Both	23
Type of contract used:	General	63%
	Tailored	37
Clause used in:	All contracts	61%
	Some contracts	39
Administrative fee required:	Yes	25%
	No	75
Only association members are permitted to use mechanism:	Yes	37%
	No	63

attorneys and reappear in partnership rather than in competition with litigation, then reconsideration should be given to the all-purpose arbitration clause. The majority of objections to commercial arbitration on the part of those who would be its friends focus on this type of clause. The general clause is seen as an expedient with which to circumvent any conceivable challenge to arbitrability which might be raised in the future. The result is that arbitration is made to encompass every dispute occurring under the contract including some for which arbitration is obviously not suited. A shift in emphasis to the careful construction of specific tailormade, individualized clauses seems to be appropriate.

Competence and compensation. Should commercial arbitrators be paid? A majority of arbitrators, both attorney and nonattorney, say yes. Warren L. Shattuck, a professor of law at the University of Washington, puts the argument this way:

In my estimation a disservice has been done arbitration by the development in some circles of the notion that this is a service which should be free. I would welcome research into this aspect of the subject and would expect the findings to disclose what seems to me to be the fact, namely, that the kind of special skill and competence in arbitrations which are essential to the long-range success of the method for resolving disputes must be paid for.

We do not claim that our research answers this question. The level of satisfaction displayed by the respondents to the questionnaire cited in Chapter II would indicate a substantial degree of satisfaction with arbitration competence at its current level. Chapter III indicates that arbitrators are generally mature, well-educated, and socially motivated people and that the special kind of competence required by arbitrators is of a highly subjective nature.

Chapter IV, however, challenges arbitrator competence as the weakest link in the entire process, and at least one judicial opinion encountered indicates that the courts are judging the entire process on the basis of the arbitrator's performance.

The roles of the arbitration panels maintained by the American Arbitration Association are increasing steadily. However, the selection process employed is not rigorous, and it is difficult to predict how well or how poorly an arbitrator will perform until he is actually arbitrating.

Can you actually buy the skills necessary to make a competent commercial arbitrator? Can you resolve the competence question by keeping on tap a small group of very competent people and paying them well?

We doubt it. Whereas currently an arbitrator averages one arbitration a year, the paid expert would have to perform more frequently. He would gain practical experience this way, but it is doubtful that he could also devote himself successfully to a business or a profession outside of arbitration. The proceeds of arbitration would have to fully support the professional arbitrator.

Could commercial arbitration afford to maintain these professionals in each of the myriad of technical specialties employed in arbitration? Such a policy would radically change the entire cost structure of arbitration and perhaps destroy its economic attractiveness. If the professional arbitrator were truly competent in his specialty, would he not find it more lucrative to practice it in industry rather than in arbitration? Commercial arbitration would end up competing for talent rather than sharing it.

It is our judgment that a program of compensation would not materially improve the general competence of arbitrators. On the contrary, it might draw "the hacks who are always available." There is evidence that recognition is more desirable than compensation. A new program established by the American Arbitration Association of presenting working arbitrators with plaques in recognition of their service is meeting with almost unanimous approval on the part of the arbitrators. Perhaps it was this desire for recognition which was being expressed when most arbitrators reported that they felt they should be paid. It was the impression of the researchers that most arbitrators observed did not desperately require the marginal income which might be derived from a token system of compensation.

WHAT CAN THE BUSINESSMAN DO?

Participation. Perhaps the strongest action a businessman can take with regard to commercial arbitration is to become an arbitrator. The only sure way of maintaining a highly competent arbitrator corps is for the most able men to devote some part of their time to this occupation. Such participation would permit a businessman to become intimately familiar with the arbitration process, evaluate its existing strengths and weaknesses, and offer suggestions for its improvement.

Investigation. The American Arbitration Association has recently developed a technique called the arbitration audit. They describe it as follows: "This service helps a corporation carry out a self-study of its contractual or other relationships—a survey of possible business controversies. This study will provide management with a valuable check-list of potential disputes, and a review as to which, if any of them, could best be submitted to arbitration." The management of a business could conduct such an audit without necessarily calling in the American Arbitration Association.[5]

---

[5] Mr. Gerald Aksen, Counsel for the American Arbitration Association, disagrees with our conclusion that an adequate arbitration audit can be conducted without the services of the Association. Nevertheless, he has graciously provided a checklist of arbitration potentials: "The following twenty-three areas are covered: Standard Form Purchase Orders; Ordinary Sales Contract-Textile Agreements; Construction Contracts; Individual Employment Contracts; Government Subcontracts; Management Systems Contracts; Stockholder Agreements; Leases; Exclusive Patent License Agreements; Exclusive Franchise and Distributorship; Partnership Agreements; International Agreements; Royalty Agreements; Factoring Agreements; Joint Use Agreements; Acquisition and Merger Agreements; Joint Ventures; Investment Agreements; Securities Transactions; Maritime Contracts; Governmental Agency Arbitration; Service Contracts; Automation Problems. There are many different problems that arise under each of these various categories necessitating different type arbitration clauses, as well as special knowledge on the part of counsel before they can adequately provide for arbitration. For each of these areas we have a broad and a narrow arbitration clause depending upon the needs of the parties concerned."

All that is necessary is a combination of businessman and attorney operating without any preconceived notions, prejudices, or misconceptions. Such an audit could begin with an evaluation of the uses described in Chapter II, and additional materials could be obtained from the American Arbitration Association, the International Chamber of Commerce, the United Nations, and the Departments of Commerce, Defense, and State.

Sponsorship. In our opinion, the most important action which a businessman could take at this time would be to mobilize active interest in arbitration. Government officials with whom we spoke commented that it is unlikely that the United States will ever participate as a signatory to a multilateral convention for the enforcement of foreign arbitral awards until the United States business community speaks out in favor of such action. Educators with whom we spoke indicated that there would be little important change in business-school curricula until the businessmen militate for some treatment of commercial arbitration. Mason Ladd, Dean, College of Law, The University of Iowa wrote the following: "One of the most effective methods to bring anything of this type before the legal profession is to include this as a subject in legal institutes, lawyer workshops, and in section meetings of bar associations. In the same light, it might be a good subject for a round table in the American Association of Law Students. . . ."

Although businessmen's associations do not exactly parallel these organizations, there are conventions, Rotary and Kiwanis meetings, and so forth. These are all forums in which commercial arbitration can be placed before businessmen for their evaluation. However, such presentations can only hope to succeed if they are done under the sponsorship of the business community.

Control. We have said that the future of commercial arbitration will be the product of a partnership between the businessman and the attorney. One of these two partners will have to make the final determination in areas where the two fall into disagreement. We believe that there is historical, economical, and logical justification for the businessman to exercise final control over the process of commercial arbitration.

THE RELATIVE IMPORTANCE OF COMMERCIAL ARBITRATION FOR BUSINESSMEN

None of the above actions will be taken unless the businessman is convinced that commercial arbitration has relative importance for him. We have described areas where it appears to have economic advantage. These have included some of the traditional, innovative, and potential domestic uses. But the true potential of commercial arbitration can only be properly appreciated from an international vantage point. It is in this area that vital and active domestic arbitration institutions and thorough individual familiarity with the process can operate to facilitate and enhance the mechanics of trade. In the international area, commercial arbitration could be of great importance to the businessman. For this reason, it demands his attention, deserves his interest, and hopefully will receive his support.

APPENDIX

APPENDIX

This appendix deals with the research performed in the preparation of this book. Its purpose is to describe the areas of investigation, the size of the populations contacted, and the response received. In addition, the objective and techniques of each research method will be indicated in order to provide the reader with a perspective on the aims and dimension of our investigations.

INDIVIDUAL GUIDANCE AND DIRECTION

Throughout the year, our group relied heavily on the advice and counsel of two men. James J. Healy, a well-known arbitrator and a professor at the Harvard Business School, participated in frequent meetings and discussions on the planning and direction of our activities. His contributions were extremely valuable, and he provided an objective sounding board for our ideas and conclusions.

The second gentleman assisting us in this endeavor was Mr. Donald B. Straus, president of the American Arbitration Association. Mr. Straus met with us frequently, took a keen interest in our work, and offered the cooperation and aid of his Association. He and the staff of his Association have made a significant contribution to our research.

INTERVIEWS

One of the primary sources of our research information has been interviews. During our investigations, over 100 men and women were personally contacted and depth interviews conducted with them. These people were from every profession and field related to commercial arbitration.

The primary emphasis was on talking with people in various segments of the legal and business communities. Additional areas in which interviews were performed included: trade and professional associations, the United Nations, the World Bank, U.S. Departments of State and Commerce, the New York Stock Exchange, judges, college law and business professors, bar associations, arbitration panels, banking institutions, and so on. These interviews were held in cities throughout the country, with primary emphasis on Boston, New York, and Washington. Various field trips have also been made to attend commercial arbitration seminars and lectures. Further, commercial arbitration seminars have been conducted by the group with professors, lawyers, and businessmen to gain a deeper knowledge of the subject.

QUESTIONNAIRES

Questionnaires as a means of data collection were used extensively. The information gathered in this manner proved to be valuable in establishing a base of data from which our research could proceed. Many of the conclusions and predictions of this book stem from the results of these questionnaires. Individual questionnaires were developed for each specific group contacted. These groups were as follows.

1. *Past arbitration participants.* Three hundred businessmen who had participated in American Arbitration Association cases during 1964 were sent questionnaires. Thirty-three percent of these past users of commercial arbitration responded by providing data on their attitudes and experiences.

2. *Nonparticipants.* Five hundred corporation presidents were selected on a random area and industry basis. These presidents were sent a questionnaire designed to establish the level of knowledge in industry concerning commercial arbitration. The response to this inquiry was approximately 35 percent.

3. *Legal community.* One hundred seventy-five lawyers from well-known law firms across the country were individually contacted. In addition, the responses from 163 corporate counsels were made available to us

by the American Arbitration Association, which had received them in reply to its own questionnaire on commercial arbitration. These questionnaires were designed to ascertain the attitudes, experiences, and viewpoints of the lawyer concerning commercial arbitration. A 60 percent response was received from this group.

4. *Trade associations.* In conjunction with the American Bar Association, City Bar Association of New York City, American Arbitration Association, and the American Society of Association Executives, a questionnaire was distributed to approximately 1,671 association executives. The questionnaire was the result of a combined effort among the groups involved, and the goal was to gather data concerning arbitration mechanisms which exist in trade groups. Replies were received from 25 percent of this mailing.

5. *Law and business schools.* The deans of 75 law and business schools were contacted and asked to comment on the role that commercial arbitration has or will have in their schools' curriculum. More than 65 percent of these deans answered our request.

6. *Arbitrators.* Some two hundred thirty commercial arbitrators, who had arbitrated frequently, were sent a questionnaire. This document was designed to obtain data on the commercial arbitration mechanism as viewed by the individual who conducts the tribunal. The response on this questionnaire approached 65 percent. In addition, a 100-man sample was taken of the American Arbitration Association's Arbitrator Panel to develop a profile of veteran arbitrators.

7. *International.* Numerous groups were contacted within the international community by sending 150 individual questionnaires to: international legal specialists, corporate international vice presidents, import-export middlemen, and international bankers. The gathering of data on the mechanism and characteristics of arbitration in an international frame was directed toward determining the differences between domestic and international commercial arbitration and the special characteristics and problems of international commercial arbitration. The response to these inquiries was 50 percent.

OTHER RESEARCH

A movie on the commercial arbitration process, produced by the American Arbitration Association, was shown to a 25-man group from the Harvard Business School Advanced Management Program. The movie was followed by a description of our research, distribution of a questionnaire, and a question-answer period. Here, an attempt was made to elicit the opinions of top managers toward commercial arbitration and its future in the business community.

Many hours were spent in researching commercial arbitration in the Harvard University libraries, especially the law and business libraries. Other sources such as the Eastman Arbitration Library of the American Arbitration Association and United Nations legal and general libraries were also utilized. An attempt has been made to review all appropriate literature on the topic.

INDEX

INDEX

M

N

P

R